Of Minitmen
&
Molly's

Of Minitmen & Molly's

North Reading Neighbors Share their Stories

Nancy Bailey Miller

Louise Anderson, Illustrator

Strathmoor Books

Copyright 2002 Nancy Bailey Miller
All rights reserved; no part of this publication may be reproduced, stored in a retrieval system, or transmitted in any form or by any means electronic, mechanical, photocopying, recording, or otherwise, without the prior written permission of Nancy Bailey Miller.

Manufactured in the United States of America
Library of Congress Control Number: 2002141250
ISBN: 1-881539-28-8
Cover design: OspreyDesign
Cover watercolor, "North Reading Common," and Illustrations: Louise Anderson
Photographer: J. D. Sloan
Copyright acknowledgments:
Town Crossings, 33 Chestnut Street, Andover, Massachusetts

All trademarks used herein are for identification only and are used without intent to infringe on the owner's trademarks or other proprietary rights.

Strathmoor Books
An imprint of Tabby House
4429 Shady Lane
Charlotte Harbor, FL 33980

Acknowledgments

All of these articles first appeared as features in the *Home Town North Reading* section of *Town Crossings* between May 1998 and May 2001. The original date appears at the end of each article to give the reader its context. Since the articles were first published, some people have moved and some have passed away. Buildings have been completed; bushes have been trimmed. After some shaping and trimming, I left these matters as they were in the original version.

Thanks to all my North Reading neighbors who shared their stories with me over the past three years—to those whose narratives appear, and to those forty whose narratives are not in this volume.

To Mark Hall for promising to buy the first book that came off the presses, and to others who have stopped me in the grocery store to ask for copies of various articles they treasured, my sincere thanks.

Thanks, also, to *Town Crossing* editors, Jen Valeri and Sharla Collier, for hiring and working with me.

For their encouragement and editing thanks to the Bartlet Street Poets, Sally Slade Warner, and to Jim and Linda Salisbury.

Contents

Introduction — xi

One: Town Center

Bill Ryer, Ryer's Store (Molly's)	15
Mark Hall, Carpenter	18
Joe and Jo, the Skating Elstons	22
Sydney Eaton, Organ Pipe Maker	26
Ed Wheeler, Farmer	30
Rowe Farm—Barry Grant, Farm Stand Proprietor	34
219 Park Street—Don and Sue Elliott's Restoration Project	37

Two: When the Trolley Went to Martins Pond

Dick and Dave Ham, Batchelder School Students in the 1940s	45
Pat and Veronica Lee, the Horseshoe Café	50
Lee and Beth Caplan, Abbott Shoe	53
Pat Romeo, Organist and Auxiliary Policewoman	57
Barbara O'Brien, Town Historian	61
The Hillview Country Club	66
Martins Pond Turtle Walk	70

Three: A Parade of Elections and Holidays

Don Roberts, Fence Viewer	77
Klaus Kubiersky, Town Moderator	80
Betty Vullo, Justice of the Peace and Town Clerk for Thirty Years	83
Martins Pond Haunted Playground	87
Apple Festival Encore	89
Phil Norris and the North Reading Community Band	91
Minitmen Again Lead the Memorial Day Parade	93
Warren Pearce Jr., Fourth of July Pyrotechnician	96
Mary Rubenstein's Fascination with Clara Louise Burnham	98

Four: Hornet Pride and Art à la Carte

Arthur Kenney, Principal Emeritus	105
Frank Carey, Baseball Coach	109
Agatha Marano, Drama Coach	112
DiFranza Designs	113
Roselin Spielman, Librarian	115
Lawrence Colford, Piano Technician	118
Scott Wheeler, Composer	121
Marie Stultz, The Treble Chorus of New England	125
Pearl Feeney-Grater, GraphoAnalyst	128

Five: Love in Action

St. Theresa Volunteers at Camp Fatima	135
Joe Sadlow, Clerk of the Works at Church Renovation	139
Fred Bauer, Seventy-Fourth Grand Master of Freemasons	143
Joan McLaughlin, Compassionate Friend for Bereaved Parents	147
Helen Eisenhaure, Quilter	149

Margaret "Peggy" Parker Turns Ninety	152
Nelda Roulliard, Artist and Author	154
Little School Ribbon Cutting	158
Fran Mague, Daniel Shay, Rufus Porter and the Flints	159

Six: Something You Can't Learn

Joe Gallagher, Hornet's Nest Sub Shop	167
Lou Greenstein, Culinary Collector	171
Ken Thomson, Cyclist	176
Katharine Barr and Billie Downing, Ninety-Nines Aviators	179
Steve Perkins, Gloucester Fisherman	183
Jack Vasapoli, Sculptor and Sax Player in Tabasco Fiasco	186
About the Author and Artist	191

Introduction

As she was working on staffing, Jen Valeri, the first editor of *Town Crossings*, contacted me in April 1998. She had seen a poster in the Flint Memorial Library announcing a poetry workshop I was giving at the library for National Poetry Month. Since I was a writer, she hoped I might know a journalist who would be willing to write a weekly feature article about North Reading for a new regional paper.

Trying to think of such a person, I mentioned this to my sister, the community news editor and columnist with a bureau of the *Sarasota Herald-Tribune* in Florida. "That job has your name all over it. Take it," urged my sister.

"I'm a poet, Linda, not a journalist. And I have no time."

"This is your job, Nancy, you need to make the time."

So began an adventure that connected me to some friends I had not seen for thirty years, and introduced me to town history I had not known.

From Joe Elston, the welder who had a roller-skating act in vaudeville; to Ed Wheeler, a farmer who invented a blue hubbard squash that would last the winter without rotting; to Joe Gallagher, the sub shop owner who starts making my cheese steak with mushrooms before I place my order—these are the diverse people that make our North Reading community. I am grateful to all of them for trusting me with their stories.

One

Town Center

Town Common—The Bandstand

Bill Ryer, Ryer's Store (Molly's)

For thirty-seven years the store was referred to as Molly's. But the sign over this small white building across from the Town Common in North Reading always read Ryer's. Established in 1912, the same year Tom Croswell opened his funeral home on the other side of the Common, Ryer's Store has always sold "dry goods." Bill Ryer Jr., who owned and ran the business from 1957 to 1992, remembers selling 300 to 400 newspapers on a typical Sunday.

"You might be surprised that pet food has always been one of our biggest sellers. Lots of cigarettes, although that market has dropped off. And milk. All the dairy products."

Bill Ryer's grandfather opened the store after moving here from Nova Scotia at the turn of the century. Originally the family lived in New York City. Loyal Tories, the Ryers fled to Canada before the Revolution to land given to them by the Crown. Over one hundred years later, when it was "safe to return," they did. Land here was cheap then. "My grandfather owned from the entrance of the high school all the way to the fire station," Bill recalls.

Born in Winchester Hospital just six years after his grandfather died, Bill has always lived in this white house on Haverhill Street. His mother, Blanche, at one time had a beauty salon in the den.

Bill's grandfather also grew cranberries. Behind his house and down the Ipswich River to the present fire station, there were bogs and a canal system that was destroyed by the 1936 flood.

"The story goes that my grandfather lugged wagons of beach sand [cranberries need sandy soil] from Salem Willows to dump here. Not sure I believe it." Bill remembers helping his grandparents harvest the cranberries. "There was a cranberry chute as big as this couch where you dropped the berries." Grates took out the stems and seeds before the berries fell into shipping crates to send to market.

When Bill was a boy, the parking lot behind the store was marsh land. You could see down to what is now Ipswich River Park. The Ryer family harvested the marsh grass to feed the livestock, and burned what was not harvested. As a result Bill and his friends were able to skate on the smooth river when it froze.

"In the 1950s the Army Corps of Engineers decided to straighten the river. They closed Haverhill Street for a year and a half which was bad for business." Jeanes' Garage, the building now occupied by Emma's Classic Cuts, especially suffered. "But the river had its own way. The sides fell in, and it eventually took its own path again."

Another government project had a more lasting effect. The New Deal came to North Reading in the 1930s when a uniformed troop of Civilian Conservation Corps (CCC) got off at the train station a block beyond Ryer's Store. Bill remembers watching them march past his house up Haverhill Street to set up barracks in Harold Parker Forest Campground.

This FDR team dredged ponds, built bridges, cleaned brush, brought in sand, and made the Parker Forest what it is today. After the state forest was cleaned up, people came by the carload, especially to swim and picnic at Berry Pond.

Many buildings were moved on log rollers in the early days of the town center. The front of Ryer's store was originally near the Reverend Daniel Putnam House on Bow Street. The house Bill lives in today was cut from the back of the store and moved across the street. The house that used to sit in its place moved to Elm Street. Behind Ryer's Store there used to be a barnyard with ducks, geese, turkeys, chickens, even a horse.

After Bill Ryer's grandfather passed away in 1920, his wife, Bertha, and her daughter, Molly, ran the place. Molly Ryer sold duck eggs at the store in addition to pumping gas out front. She kept livestock and thirteen cats. Ryer's Store was even the post office for a short period of time, Molly serving as postmistress. Her brother (Bill Ryer's dad) ran the mail route on the west side of town.

"It was Rural Free Delivery (RFD), not pony express. No, he left his horse at home," jokes Bill. Nothing seemed to change location so frequently as North Reading's post office. At one time Sadie Wickum ran it from Damon Tavern. Later you picked up your mail in Jones

Brothers' Store where Video Outpost is today. Ryer also remembers the post office on Bow Street where chiropractor Beth Kahmi now has her offices.

Molly stopped pumping gas during World War II when Bill was in Naples, Italy, in the infantry.

"Ashamed to say, I never actually got assigned to an outfit. I arrived in April after training in Blanding, Florida, and the war ended in May. It took me longer to get home than the time I served."

Given a choice to return by boat or plane, Bill thought plane might be faster. Was he wrong! First the soldiers flew from Rome to Casa Blanca where they waited a week because of the back up. Then they shipped him via Dakar, Africa, to Belem, Brazil, a port at the mouth of the Amazon, where a Caribbean hurricane caused delay. From Brazil he flew to San Juan and finally to Blanding, where he had begun. Still on furlough, he was to be shipped to the Pacific, "but the Japanese heard I was coming and pulled out of the war," he says with a smile.

Out of the Army, Bill finished his schooling at Bentley College and went to work as an accountant for Sealtest. After a few years in Worcester, Burlington, Vermont, and Watertown, New York, he decided to return to North Reading in 1953. That year Aunt Molly had a serious illness and needed his help to run the store. "I fell into it. Got in the habit." In 1957 he purchased Ryer's Store from Molly.

"I had some wonderful people working for me over the years: my mother, Blanche; my cousin Helen Eisenhaur, and her mother, Beulah; Millie Cameron, who later cared for my father until he died in 1990. Then there was Nancy Kenty, Angie Pepper and Joan Coffill." Joan worked for Ryer for twenty-five years. "I never applied for the job. I was just in the store talking with my friend Helen Eisenhaur one day, and Bill asked me to stay."

"Every day was a different day with him," remembers Millie Cameron. "Billy was generous to the whole town. A true friend. To this day I respect him."

Bill loved being in the store. He loved to talk and joke with the customers. "People don't have a reason to come into a small store unless you give them one. Being friendly helps," says Bill.

On three occasions people came into the store for the wrong reasons. Ryer remembers three robberies—all unsuccessful. Held up at gunpoint, Molly chased the man and woman out with her umbrella. "Molly wasn't giving up anything," remembers Bill. Cousin Helen dealt with two attempted robberies. Both times her piercing scream drove the would-be robbers from the store.

From 1961 to the early 1970s Bill Ryer served on the North Reading School Committee. During that time, school committee members came to the store to have Bill sign schedules and payroll. Politics was sometimes the topic at the cash register.

Bill served under three superintendents: Dr. Francis X. O'Donoghue, Dr. George Quinn and Dr. Albert Benson. "I ran for office with retired Superintendent J. T. Hood, a distinguished gent. I think people actually thought they were voting for my father. He knew everyone from his mail route."

Controversy was swirling at the time; the town was growing rapidly, and the school budget was exploding. In 1966 the board hired Dr. Benson from Darien, Connecticut. "He made some radical changes. Once in a public meeting he said in frustration, 'You know, running the school department is not like running the neighborhood store.' I got a kick out of that!"

—September 11, 1998

Mark Hall, Carpenter

"Mark wanted to be a carpenter since he was old enough to walk," remembered his father, Gordon Hall. "At thirteen or so he'd get home from school and see a loose shingle on the house. Before I was home from work he'd get out a ladder and fix it." At age five, Mark's first building project was a fort in the woods behind 276 Elm Street. He went on to build ten tree houses and forts after his family moved to 12 Upton Avenue in 1967.

With six children to house and a penchant for antique dwellings, Gordon and Pauline Hall had always dreamed of owning the Upton homestead, built in 1702 by Francis Nurse, the son of Rebecca Nurse, the first witch to be executed at the Salem Witch Trials.

Amos Upton moved into the house in 1753, having the choice of the Nurses' white colonial or the Turner Farm on Elm Street. Amos gave the latter to his older brother, Joseph, and chose the former for himself. Two hundred forty-four years later Mark Hall came to own both these houses and made the same choice for his family—to live at 12 Upton Avenue. In the 1940s and 1950s, Harold was the last Upton to live in this family home. At the time, the lumberyard on nearby Chestnut Street was Upton Lumber before it belonged to the Moynihans. Housed in the carriage house across from the windmill and the old slaughterhouse, the Upton Lumber trucks accessed the lumberyard via a drive that cut across the current soccer fields.

Gordon Hall made seven visits to the Upton property before he convinced the Hobart family to sell it to him. "We were counting votes in the 1962 election," recalls Gordon, "We counted them by hand then. Had to be two Democrats and two Republicans present. Kitty's Restaurant brought in ham sandwiches at midnight. We were usually there all night before we finished."

Earl Hobart was counting next to Gordon and introduced himself. Said he lived over on Upton Avenue.

"There's a house I'd like to own on Upton Ave.," said Gordon, "but I understand the person who lives there would never sell."

"Which one is it?"

"Last house up on the left," said Gordon.

"Well, as it happens it is for sale. That's my house."

Earl did not really want to sell the house; it was his wife who was pushing the idea. But after a visit or two, and after Gordon admitted he really could not afford the house, Earl's attitude toward Gordon softened. Mark, who was seven at the time, was the only one of his siblings who saw the house before its purchase.

"I knew when I visited the house that day that someday it was going to be mine," said Mark. "I guess that is why I wanted to go to work so young—to save money for that house."

When he was ten, Mark worked for Ed Wheeler at the cabbage farm at the foot of Central Street. "We weeded mostly, my brother Jeff and I." Eddie Wheeler rented fields in Rowley, and Mark recalls riding up Route 95 on the tailgate of Wheeler's 1963 Chevy wagon, dragging his feet on the hot top. "I think he paid us twenty-five cents an hour," said Mark.

Later, Ed Carlson, a builder who owned a sawmill at the Middleton end of Route 62, needed help clearing brush at Hayward Farms. Mark and his friend Gary Baxter worked for Ed Carlson when they were still teenagers.

"Sometimes I worked for my father in his sheet metal business, but I also had my own painting business when I was twelve."

Ronny Piercy, his neighbor, had a van and a driver's license and Mark hired him to paint when the jobs were out of town. "We painted half a dozen houses, Hilltop Nursery School, and my grandmother's house in Peabody." Gary Baxter and Mark also painted Roy Conway's home in Andover; Roy was North Reading High School's athletic director at the time. "I painted that windmill in our yard for three dollars. Not easy, but at least it was laying down," Mark said.

"Mark was always a levelheaded kid," said his father. "You didn't worry. He could be trusted." Before he was old enough to have a license he turned over a tractor he was driving and almost killed himself. "I'm not sure I authorized the driving of the tractor at age fourteen," said his father, "but then maybe I did. Mark was careful."

Mark's fort carpentry got him into some trouble in his early teens; in retrospect there is a touch of irony in the escapade. Having run out of old crates his dad brought home from work, Mark walked through the woods to Moynihan Lumber yard one afternoon to price some supplies. Unfortunately he learned a single board cost three dollars; that was a lot more than he could spend.

A friend of his brother's was out in the yard working a forklift. Mark asked him if there were any scrap wood, would he mind putting it aside for him as long as the lumberyard was just going to throw it away. In reply, the young employee suggested Mark just take some; he did not need much.

Mark and his neighborhood pals were nailing the boards into the fort when a North Reading police cruiser pulled into the yard a few hours later.

"Who's in charge here?" the officer asked.

"I am," said Mark. So, the police took him for a ride in the cruiser to talk with Mike Moynihan, the owner of Moynihan Lumber."

"Do you want us to arrest him?" the policeman asked Mike Moynihan.

"I think not," was the response. "He might be a good customer some day."

With a thriving construction business in North Reading today, Mark is, indeed, a very good customer.

After he got his diploma from the Northeast Metropolitan Regional Vocational School in 1979, Mark got his federal ID number and began renovating and building houses. Mark has built probably fifteen new homes in North Reading, the newest part of Turner Farms subdivision being a major project for him in the 1990s. He has renovated literally thousands of homes in the area. Mark has never had to advertise; all his business is referral.

"I enjoyed designing those houses on Turner Farm—authentic chimneys, granite stairs. I got the nickname of Santa Claus there because I could not resist putting in the extras."

Richard "Nick" Nickerson really taught Mark the building trade. "From him I learned restoration, old house stuff. Lyman Fancy, Gordon Mills, my father and especially Mr. Nickerson taught me craftsmanship and good work ethics. Mr. Nickerson showed me how old houses are put together, how old buildings should look. The old methods are still the best." Mark's role models believed in a day's work for a day's pay. They convinced him that the quality of what does not show is just as important as that which does.

From age twelve Mark Hall worked by Nick's side. After Mark got his driver's license he remembers leaving the voc school in his '62 Chevy, listening to the Beach Boys as he drove to a construction site in Wilmington or to Sadie Wedge's house on Park Street East, where he also learned restoration techniques from Nick Nickerson.

Authentic restoration is Mark Hall's passion. When Raymond Tumer's daughter, Joan Fairweather, had been told her father's farmhouse and barn needed to come down, Mark quite agreed. "I bought the Turner Farm with the idea of tearing it down. Too costly to fix." But after living in it for a few months, he felt the need to preserve its charm.

Outside there was very little done: a new roof, paint, new farmer's porch, and wooden shutters to replace the vinyl.

The inside, however, Mark completely restored, from center chimney to thumb latch door handles. Linda Thomas and Boyce Rensberger bought Turner Farm in 1997, and it was on the historic home tour Gloria Mastro organized for Thanksgiving weekend 1999.

"Turner Farmhouse was not a profitable project," said Mark, "but we had a vision."

Mark and his mother Pauline, an artist with an eye for interior design, had a vision for the old slaughterhouse on the Upton property as well. "We always talked about converting it and had begun to restore it as a barn. My mother liked the way it was coming out."

Moving the rotted building, which in Mark's youth had housed Chubby the horse and Ginny, a boarding pony, the Upton slaughterhouse became Gordon and Pauline's unique retirement home. The living room still has the hooks and track in the ceiling where the hog carcasses hung, and the wheel pulley on the west wall that lifted the animals. The master bathroom is the former walk-in cooler, which in earlier times was insulated with hand-sawed sawdust.

Having purchased it in April 1999, Mark Hall has transformed the Elston Welding Building into a place for his business. A large structure, it also houses a welding business and another carpentry shop.

"I wanted it to have the country town look. As we were planning the renovation, it began to look like a Grange hall in Dover, New Hampshire, that my family used to go to when I was a kid." A friend of Mark's convinced him to put on copper gutters. Self-cleaning, they will never rot. "I've never used copper gutters before, but I figure that building will be there in 200 years. What's a few extra dollars now?"

In the fall of 1998, Mark donated his time and expertise to move a small cobbler's shop, which town historian Barbara O'Brien found at the back of the Riverdale Cemetery, to the Putnam house property. "I got my form contractor, my mason and my painter to donate their time. Moynihan's donated the lumber." Emotionally invested in the historic center of the town, Mark as well as his father and his children have all attended the Batchelder School.

"If I ever hit Megabucks and didn't have to make a living, I'd like to start at the center of North Reading and buy up all the old houses and restore them. That would be my dream," said Mark.

—January 21, 2000

Joe and Jo, the Skating Elstons

Mark Hall's construction vehicles are a daily presence on Park Street in front of the Elston Welding Building, closed since October 1999. This past fall, at the age of eighty-two, Joe Elston stopped welding, a business he had run in town since 1949. Prior to his buying that lot for $800 in 1956, Elston's welding business stood across the street in a smaller, still standing, cement structure. Before building a home on that corner lot, Joe, his wife and two children lived in an adjacent twenty-seven foot trailer.

"I decided to retire when I was lying on the floor of my shop and couldn't get up," said Joe Elston. "The arthritis was so bad I couldn't lift my arms over my head. It was time to quit."

"If that didn't happen he'd still be working," piped up his wife of almost sixty years. Joe Elston met Josephine Araszkiewicz at the Canobie Lake Roller Skating Rink in 1936. "That was the best rink in the area at the time. The rink is still there, but it hasn't been used in years," said Elston. At the time Joe was a professional skater; soon Jo became part of the act. As "The Skating Comets," the duo first appeared at rinks and nightclubs in Nahant, Quincy, Lawrence, Lowell and Cambridge. In 1938, their first road trip to Canada lasted six weeks; they played all the coaling towns.

"We went back fifty years later and couldn't find a single theater," recalled Joe.

"Joe was known as the fastest spinner around," said his wife. Performed on a ten-foot-square mat, their most spectacular tricks featured spinning. In one trick, Jo had a match in her mouth which she took from her shoe as her husband spun her around, lowering her closer and closer to the floor. Then *poof!* The theater manager would kill the lights as Jo Elston struck the match on the floor. "I often had a very sore nose," she said.

"You do what ever is necessary to please the audience." Joe said with a smile.

The Elstons played carnivals, circuses, nightclubs and private shows. On many occasions they worked with Sammy Davis Jr., his father and his uncle. Known at the time as The Will Mastin Trio, the tap-dancing brothers often passed young Sammy off as a midget because one had to be twenty-one to work the nightclubs. The Elstons have also played nightclubs with Frank Fontaine, a comedian you may remember as Crazy Googenheimer on "The Jackie Gleason Show."

"A lot of performers spend their life in the business and are never more than a good act," said Jo.

In the old days there were nightclubs in every town; one perfected an act locally. "I used to pick her up by the ankle and throw her around," said Joe, "but that was too hard a trick. What you need is something flashy that does not take so much effort," he said.

How did they learn to swing from nooses around their necks and spin holding a partner by one leg? "Joe invented the routines," recalled his wife. "He just picked it up." He tried some of the spins on ice skates, but never had figure skates, only hockey skates.

In the 1930s Joe Elston was working in the mills in Andover's Shawsheen Village, but the work was not stable so he performed regularly on the skates. He did collect unemployment insurance once for seven weeks at seven dollars per week. With that $49 he was able to purchase his first car, a 1929 black Ford. "You could get a Ford in any color in those days, as long as it was black," he joked.

In 1940 Joe and Jo were married, changing the name of their act from "The Skating Comets" to "The Skating Elstons." Appearing on a Pat Rooney poster for the Gay Nineties Restaurant, the Elstons promised "thrills, spills, laffs."

Jo Elston fondly recalled her lilac and Vatican purple costume with red sequins that she had crafted for the Gay Nineties routine. "That costume cost me $350," she said. "All handmade."

One costume she made herself had 10,000 blue sequins. "When the spotlight hit those sequins—what a flash!" she said.

The Skating Elstons never lowered themselves to play at the Silver Dollar Bar, the red-light district establishment that heralded Boston's famed Combat Zone. Instead, they had gigs at Symphony Hall, The Boston Garden and The Latin Quarter, which was owned by Barbara Walters' father at the time.

"We never drank with the customers. It was an athletic act—you don't drink," said Joe.

"Many of the entertainers had drinking problems," Jo added. "We once worked with a knife-thrower who drank. His partner had a few scars!"

In 1941, to help the war effort, Joe Elston, who had originally trained as a mechanic, made a career change. "We closed at the Swan Club in Philly and booked seven weeks in Boston," he recalled. After parking their trailer at his mother's, Joe took the train to Portland, Maine, arriving at South Portland Shipyard to find long lines of prospective workers.

"Where do I find out about the welding business?" Joe asked a guard.

"Right this way."

After seven days in welding school, Joe began work on the 800-foot Liberty ships the yard had promised to England, which were so critical to the Allied war effort. "I showed up in a suit and white shirt," recalled Joe. "I was an entertainer. I didn't have any work clothes or tools."

While welding Joe wore leather gloves he had to replace every few days. Sparks and metal gobs would fall on his shoes and burn his clothes; he still has scars. Production welding paid $9.60 a day with time and a half on weekends. Workers got a bonus of eighty cents per pound to burn 3/16-inch wire. "I could burn thirty pounds in a day and make $24. We often worked twelve-hour shifts," said Joe.

The war effort over, Joe and his wife returned to skating. In their 1947 Roadmaster Buick with a straight 8 engine, they pulled their trailer from Minnesota to Iowa to South Dakota, sometimes for six months at a time. But soon there were two small children traveling with them. "I skated until I was six months pregnant with Carolyn," volunteered Jo.

Their agent wanted them to join the USO and do shows for the military, but their son's early days were fraught with medical complications and surgeries. Time to stay put in North Reading.

They shared their last Midwest tour with two other North Reading acts: The Howard Fuller Trio and Webb and Brooks. Howard Fuller was the stage name for Howard Ying, a good friend of the Elstons who had built a house on Mt. Vernon Street. Webster Taylor (stage name Gary Webb) and Florence Brooks also owned a home in North Reading. Gary was a comedian and dancer; Florence played the accordion.

It was Gary who actually got Joe out of Vaudeville and back into the welding business. Gary had been disappointed with the work of a welder on Route 62 near Middleton. This businessman was the kind who closed his shop at 4:00 P.M. even if he only had five more minutes of work to finish the job. "This welder actually advised me, 'Don't do the job too good; they won't come back.' Now, this is not my thinking," said Joe. "I always want the job to be finished right. I don't want it to break."

Frustrated by the poor welding on his car, Gary said to Joe, "If I knew as much about welding as you do, I'd be in the welding business."

Continuing his skating career on the side until the middle 1950s, Joe became primarily a welder. "Isn't much I haven't welded," he said. Joe has welded the damaged canopy on top of the North Reading water tower and welded repairs to the Anderson Brothers' Hog

Farm machinery in Wilmington. He has replaced the bottom of oil tanks in buildings under Boston skyscrapers and fixed North Reading DPW trucks. Joe has put trailer hitches on cars and fixed pipelines to the fish tanks at Sailor Tom's Restaurant. Joe even made an aluminum xylophone stand for Salve Cavicchio that weighed only twelve pounds.

"I always had to put his clothes through the washer twice," said his wife. Then I'd rinse the tub by itself." The welding business is a dirty operation, hot metal flying around, lots of dust. Just the other day, Mark Hall asked Joe Elston to walk across the street and see his progress with the building renovation. "He certainly has cleaned the place up," said Joe.

How will he spend his retirement? "Not a lot of things I would like to do that I haven't done," said Joe. "I go clamming regularly with friends in Ipswich. I guess I'd like to take a trip to Alaska."

—*July 5, 1999*

Sydney F. Eaton, Organ Pipe Maker

If you live in North Reading you undoubtedly have had oc-casion to wave to an elderly man with a jaunty hat and four-in-hand tie, riding an old, green, balloon-tire bike. Lashed to the back of this bike is a large wooden milk box with a red reflector the size of a dinner plate. This gentleman always has his pants legs clipped to protect them from the bicycle chain; his basket is sometimes filled with groceries, sometimes pussy willows or forsythia he has just cut. He rides in all seasons; he salutes and smiles.

Sydney F. Eaton has lived in the same gray house on Chestnut Street for ninety-one years, except for the winter about ten years ago when his house burned, and it was necessary for him to spend time with relatives in Connecticut. The week of the fire, Syd Eaton asked his neighbors Gordon Hall, Gordon Mills and Ginny Mills to secure the place. The fire having been caused by a space heater, Cyrus Mugford refurbished the interior and installed central heating. "Mr. Eaton and I corresponded all that winter," remembers Gordon Hall. "I hadn't written letters since I was in service. It was kind of nice."

Syd Eaton was born in North Reading in the house on Chestnut Street. He claims that the homestead previously belonged to Seth

Fowle, the man who discovered and perfected Coca-Cola, and who also owned the Fowle Blade Company that manufactured hand saws. Syd attended North Reading Public Schools through grade eight, the last grade offered locally at the time. Later he had two years of industrial school in Lowell. Always interested in science, at age fourteen he apprenticed himself to Dr. Hilliard, a research scientist for Kodak. "Dr. Hilliard showed me the first colored picture I ever saw," said Syd. "He taught me everything about developing pictures, and warned me to always be very careful mixing chemicals."

Ed Wheeler, a long time neighbor of Syd's, remembers that years ago Syd was quite a figure skater in his red knickers, attire that was popular in that day. Cars would slow down on Park Street to watch Syd's fancy skating in the meadows on the west side of Central Street before the area became swampy and overgrown. Today Syd regularly rides his bicycle to the train station in Reading on his way to Boston to skate at a rink.

Harold Richardson, whose father, Roy, opened his gas station on Winter Street in 1924, has clear memories of Syd's 1927 Model-T Ford. Always shined so that you could see your reflection on the hood, the car drove up to the pump every day so that Syd could top off the tank.

"Roy, give me a pint of ethyl (high test) and a pint of regular," Syd would request. There was an elaborate hood ornament, which Harold Richardson suspects Syd created from organ pipe materials. In the late 1930s Ed Wheeler remembers Syd sold the Model T to some kids on Franklin Street for four dollars. Without a license plate they were detained by the police as they took the car back to Reading. Ed Wheeler, on the other hand, thinks Bob Doyle bought the car. Harold also recalls that Syd was a fine ballroom dancer, self-taught. Attending all the weekly dances at the Grange, Syd would dance every dance. By his own admission an athlete, Syd also trained more than once for the Boston Marathon, but he never ran the race because of commitments to his work installing and tuning pipe organs all over the world.

A gentleman to the core, Syd routinely presents flowers to town secretaries, shopkeepers in Reading, post office employees and total strangers. "I try to be nice to the ladies," said Syd, "and they don't object. A woman just wants someone to treat her decent. I don't socialize. Don't like it a bit." Syd's longtime employer, mentor and friend, Ernest M. Skinner, also was accustomed to giving ladies a red rose. "Mr. Skinner got more than one organ contract by talking with the ladies. He was a good salesman," said Syd.

For twenty-five of the seventy-five years he worked making organ pipes, Syd worked for E. M. Skinner, the renowned organ builder. "Organs, music and mechanics have been my life," said Syd. Sydney F. Eaton is mentioned in the acknowledgments of the Organ Historical Society book by Dorothy J. Holden, *The Life and Work of Ernest M. Skinner*. Dorothy Holden is not the only organ historian with whom Syd Eaton has shared his memories, however.

Barbara Owen, organist at the First Religious Society of Newburyport for thirty-five years, and first and present president of the Organ Historical Society, first met Syd Eaton in the 1970s when she was writing *The Organ in New England*. At that time, he was still working at the Dennison Organ Pipe Factory in Reading. "God only knows how many pipes he made over a lifetime," said Barbara. During the latter part of the 19th century there were three or four organ companies in Reading. The Samuel Pierce Organ Pipe Company, established in the 1840s, became Dennison Organ Pipe Company at the turn of the century.

"Syd Eaton would have been trained as an apprentice," Barbara suspects. "That is still the only way to learn the organ pipe business. Syd is an old-time gentleman, one of the last of the old-time organ technicians."

Over the years, Syd's organ pipe work took him to California, Duke University, Washington, D.C., and France. "I was the chief engineer to make pipes for the Washington Cathedral. If you ever go in there you should walk in and remain silent. Beautiful tapestries, and what a wonderful acoustic!" Syd personally made ten of the stops (with sixty-one pipes per stop) of the 225 total stops for the Hammond Castle organ built for John Hays Hammond in Gloucester; E. M. Skinner and John Hays Hammond were good friends.

Syd also became friends with Albert Einstein, who had more than a passing curiosity about the organ installation at Princeton Chapel when Syd was working there for E. M. Skinner. A physics professor at Princeton at the time, Albert Einstein was also a decent organist and, reputedly, a mediocre violinist.

Because of his work with E. M. Skinner, Syd knew Mr. Bose of Bose Radio fame, and also Boston Pops conductor Arthur Fiedler.

"He was a scientist, Mr. Skinner, a scientist very deep into the science of tone," said Syd. "He had to have perfection." The development of the English horn and French horn stops reflected Skinner's interest in developing organs that sounded more orchestral.

How does Syd fill his hours today? He is an avid gardener, with rakes and trowels neatly hung on pegs in his front entry. In addition to his trips on the Reading train to skate in Boston, he takes the train to visit his doctors at Massachusetts General Hospital for his yearly checkups. "The hospital food is outstanding; those dietitians know what you need. Carbohydrates, proteins, potassium. You know, everybody is a chemical factory. Last week I got the special chicken salad sandwich and a cup of black tea."

Syd also regularly visits the Science Museum. "I still have so much to learn."

Syd often spends his evening working on clocks. "Last week I worked on this mahogany wave-front clock for twenty-four hours. I forgot to eat dinner, actually. You know, the brain can overcome the appetite when you have a project; now that's a fact." The clocks are made of mahogany, maple and walnut; the pendulums, made of brass or gold, he designs to swing for two years. There are parts for twelve or more of them on his kitchen table. On a recent visit to Mass General, Syd presented one of the clocks to a nurse there. "She takes good care of me."

" 'Are you looking for a date?' she said. 'No, I'm a little too old for that.' I said."

He has three Victorian victrolas that wind up on the side. He retrieved them from the dump maybe twenty-five years ago, refinished the cabinets, cleaned and realigned the mechanical parts. One has a tungsten steel needle; on another he has used whale oil as a lubricant. The interior of one victrola cabinet is lined with pieces of ivory, producing, he points out, not a penetrating, but a floating tone. Of his collection of over 400 records including Lili Pons, John Philip Sousa and Guy Lombardo, he remarked, "These give more pleasure than a radio." Syd plays the Westminster chimes on one, a Sousa march on the other.

To what does he attribute his longevity? "I don't use salt or sugar. Don't smoke. No booze. No cussing. I take care of myself; only drink my own well water. I stay to myself and mind my own business."

—April 23, 1999

Ed Wheeler, Farmer

Imagine. A poultry show in the upstairs of the Town Hall, now the Flint Memorial Library! In the 1930s, with thirty poultry farms and twenty dairy farms in North Reading, the annual poultry event awarded blue ribbons to the best hens, based on production. The Topsfield Fair now hosts these events.

"You see, a hen's value depends on how many eggs she lays from a pound of grain. The Rhode Island Reds were the most popular," recalls Ed Wheeler who farmed North Reading land for over sixty years.

Ed's grandfather came to Lynn, Massachusetts, from New Jersey in 1900 to work in the shoe industry. Living near Lynn's Wyoma Square and raising nine children, Harry Wheeler kept a cow for extra income. When Ed's father, Charles, was a young man, Grandpa Harry bought a dairy farm in West Peabody. That Russell Street location becoming too small in the early 1920s, Harry and two of his seven sons, Robert and Charles, purchased Elms Farm from the Omstead family in North Reading.

In 1924, Ed was born in the back section of what today is Rowe Farm at 283 Elm Street. His three sisters were also born in that house. "The farm had its own bottling plant, ice house and thirty cows. My father delivered the milk to Lynn in a Stanley Steamer milk truck built by the Stanley brothers in Newton, Massachusetts." Ed's grandfather had a touring car called a Wescott with "Isinglass curtains," precursor to roll-down glass windows.

When Ed was a boy, Wendell "Ted" Crosby had his barbershop at Dutton's Corner, where Elm Street, Washington Street and Orchard Drive meet. Twenty-five cents paid for a haircut, and thirty-five cents included a shave. Before the days of hydraulic barber chairs, Ed Wheeler remembers Ted putting a board across the arms of the barber chair for Ed's first haircut.

"Across the street Harold Turner's wife, Anne, had a little variety store and ice cream parlor. Five cents for chocolate or vanilla." Ed's favorite was a five-cent bag of "old fashioneds"—chocolate-coated peppermint, probably made by Necco in Cambridge. "Mrs. Turner also kept hens in the cellar," he said.

Before Ed attended school he remembers how Arthur Burditt, who took the mail to Reading in a stage coach, would give him a package of pastel Necco wafer mints each time he delivered the groceries to the farm.

When he was only about four years old, Ed was already interested in trucks and farming. Having asked his father for a toy truck, and not getting it right away, young Ed took the key from the ignition of his father's truck—no one ever took keys out of cars back then—and buried it.

"I figured if they could plant seed and get corn, I could do the same with a key and get a truck. I was an innovator from the start," he mused.

Ed purchased his first car, a Model T, when he was only twelve. Already driving farm tractors, he did not yet have a license. Since Swan Pond Road was, and still is, a private way, Ed could drive up behind his grandfather's property. "I didn't have that car a week before I broke my wrist cranking it. It was spring before we got the car going."

At thirteen Ed bought a 1929 Model A from Allen Sweetser for five dollars. "I got to know his boy from swimming in the Ipswich River. You could buy any used car in town for five dollars. Offer anything less, it was an insult," he said.

Ed rode the bus to first grade at the Batchelder School. Sharing a classroom with forty children, his classmates included Billy Ryer Jr., Johnny Mentus, Barbara Normine Tobey and Donald Rich. After ninth grade there was a graduation in the Town Hall auditorium, the same space that earlier welcomed the poultry shows. Across the street and up the hill from the Town Hall, the Third Meeting House (Building on the Common) was often a place for dances and husking bees. The Grange, a civic and agricultural organization, met upstairs, while the American Legion, primarily Veterans of World War I, held their dances on the first floor. Husking bees were popular in the fall. After the corn was picked by hand, it had to be husked to dry. The dances were a celebration of the harvest, but also an opportunity to get the husking done. Whoever husked an ear of corn with red kernels got to dance with the lady of his choice. As the automobile became more prevalent, some of these hometown events were less well attended.

After finishing ninth grade at Batchelder School, Ed enrolled in the machinist course at Somerville Vocational School. Already, he was tinkering with engines and raising sweet corn on the side. To go to school Ed took the bus to Reading, the train to North Station, the elevated to Sullivan Square and then picked up the street car to Broadway in Somerville. "It took almost two hours to get home. That discouraged me," he said.

Ed was only sixteen and a half when his father was killed in a tractor farm accident. "It was April 4th, and we were going to spread cow manure the next day. They loaded the truck the night before, but being wet, the manure froze over night." Since the manure would not slide out of the truck body, his father went to check. The extra weight of the frozen load snapped the rod in the hydraulic mechanism so that the bin came down quickly and killed his father instantly. "I was up to Looney Hill (at the end of Oakland Drive) plowing a garden. Mother had driven to Sears to buy Easter clothes for the girls. We went looking for her, but could not find her."

After his father died, Ed's mother went to work at Boston Blacking Chemical (now BOSTIK) in Middleton, a company that originally made the black finish for wood stoves. Replacing his father in the farming business, Ed joined his Uncle Rob, who was fourteen years his senior, raising corn, squash and cabbage.

For two reasons Ed and his uncle rented fields for their crops rather than buying them. First they reasoned that an acre of land in North Reading was ninety percent swamp or ledge and ten percent plantable. Why own the whole farm? Secondly, it had taken Ed's grandfather thirteen years to sell his Elm Street dairy farm, asking $40 an acre. In 1946 Harry Wheeler finally sold it to Carl Bigham Sr. who developed the land with modest homes on Erwin, Virginia and Bigham Roads. Ed was hesitant to have his capital tied up that way.

At the peak of his productivity Ed farmed 125 acres of land in North Reading, Rowley, Georgetown, Tewksbury, North Andover, Haverhill and Newburyport. "By renting the land I could pick land with a mixture of soils. That way my eggs weren't all in one basket."

He sold his squash and cabbage wholesale to A&P, First National, Economy Grocery Stores (Stop & Shop today), Star Market, Purity and DeMoulas. He still has a receipt from First National Stores dated January 1966, for 1,000 pounds of blue hubbard squash at three and a half cents per pound, fifteen crates of butternut squash at $250 per crate and 400 pounds of cut butternut for nine cents a pound. How could he sell so much squash in the winter and spring? "Prices strengthen as you get into spring," he explained. "If it rots there is no profit at all. Some seed comes with disease. To weed out the disease, I selected seed from squash that lasted the longest. Unfortunately as I was improving it, the demand for blue hubbard went down. People preferred squash that was not so hard to prepare. My largest blue hubbard hybrid weighed seventy-five pounds."

Ed also has receipts for supplies his father bought from Frank Spinney in Haverhill and Fred E Smith, Inc. in Reading. In 1938, the Wheelers purchased Sure Crop bean seeds, Super Snowball cauliflower, cucumber, rutabaga, two tons of fertilizer and two quarts of crow repellant.

Ed remembered his father's transactions with H. K. Webster in Lawrence, which is still in business today. "Sometimes they put prizes in the grain bags. My mother got a set of sterling in a grain bag once: knife, fork and spoon. The grain bags held 100 pounds. They were mostly floral print. My mother made pillowcases out of them. You didn't waste anything."

Ed bought his land at the foot of Central Street in the early 1950s from Sydney Eaton's father, Arthur, one of the best carpenters in town. At ninety-one, Sydney is still a neighbor of the Wheelers. "We had been renting Arthur Eaton's land. Paid him seventy-five dollars a year, which about covered his taxes." One afternoon Ed dropped in on Arthur Eaton and asked if he'd sell three acres.

"How much you give me?" asked Arthur.

"Five hundred dollars," offered Ed. This was a lot of money considering his grandfather's Elm Street farm had gone unsold thirteen years at $40 an acre. Arthur was happy to sell. Today most of that land is the maintenance staging area for the Ipswich River Park. The cabbage fields on the west side of Central Street became single-family house lots.

On that land Ed built 1 Central Street with ninety percent lumber felled in North Reading near Pleasant Street and milled at what was the Curtis Saw Mill on the Middleton line. In the meantime a friend had introduced him to Ellen, who was to become his wife. "How many brides have a new house to move into when they marry?" asked Ed.

"I didn't marry Ed because he was a farmer. I married him for love. Farming was never easy. At least I didn't think it was ever easy," she said.

What were some of the challenges of being a farmer? Ed mentions the unpredictability of weather. He would listen to the radio reports regularly, but in the end, "You really did your own forecasting," he said.

The problem of pollution led Ed to Salem District Court in the early 1950s. In one particular field he rented in Georgetown, the butternut squash runner vines were curling. After speaking with a plant pathologist at the University of Massachusetts, Ed surmised it was the fumes from the herbicide vapors that the town had sprayed on roadside poison ivy that was causing the wilting. Ed won his day in court with a settlement of $4,000 to cover the cost of 1,000 boxes of lost squash.

Ed's children, Nancy and Charles, both worked for him before going to college. A certified mechanical engineer today, Charles said, "I laughed every day I worked with Dad."

"Farmers work seven days a week," said Ed. "My philosophy was, if something happens that's out of your control, why cry over it?"

—*April 7, 2000*

Rowe Farm—Barry Grant, Farmstand Proprietor

What motivates a young person who has spent two-thirds of his life in Los Angeles to come back to North Reading and open a farm stand to sell pumpkins? We're talking about a young man who has studied international business, has sold his own line of clothing in London, and who was a currency broker in L. A. While in Newport Beach, he even began his career as a stand-up comic at Laff Stop, one of the nation's first comedy clubs.

Barry Grant II admits he has never been a nine-to-five person. At age sixteen he worked as a stagehand in Disneyland, which led to set construction for television commercials. "I worked for a gentleman who did the commercial sets for Isuzu Impreza, Honda Passports, every make and model really, and toy commercials like Hot Wheels and Barbie Dolls," explained Barry. For a period of time he set up the sound and lighting equipment for some road bands—Madonna, Janet Jackson and U-2, to name a few.

Completing his international business studies in California, he landed a job trading currency on the foreign exchange. To sell the British pound and the German Deutsche mark, Barry had to arrive at work at 6:00 A.M. when Wall Street opened on the East Coast.

Nights were short after working the comedy clubs. "The money was good, but the environment was too sterile. The pace too fast. Too much pressure," remembered Barry.

He moved to London to work with two friends from South Africa who owned an art gallery named Scar. In the very fashionable Camden Town district, they marketed mostly metal sculptures that looked industrial. "I did a line of apparel for them not unlike Mossimo or Stussy, clothing made popular on the West Coast by *Surfer* magazine." The clothing line did well, but the South African partners did not get along with one another; the business folded, and Barry headed back to the states.

When he left London two years ago, there were several reasons Barry decided to resettle in North Reading rather than return to Los Angeles. "For one thing, L. A. was really saturated with stand-up comics; I was ready to leave the fast lane for a bit. I had roots here in North Reading," Barry said. He had lived on Haverhill Street just south of the Baptist Church until he was eleven. In addition, Grandpa Dana Rowe Sr. was still living in the big farmhouse on Elm Street. "I wanted to spend some time with my grandfather."

Dana and Neva Rowe had a farm stand "off-and-on" over the fifty years they lived at Rowe Farm on Route 62. "At one time Granddad provided all the cabbages for the slaw at Sailor Tom's Restaurant in Reading." Did you ever wonder why that large white boat was moored on Franklin Street behind Marshalls?

Helen Bigham remembers eating at Sailor Tom's in the 1930s. "It was very nautical—ropes, anchors, life preservers." And great coleslaw, apparently.

Dana Rowe Sr. and his wife, Neva, purchased the farm on Elm Street on May 26, 1947, from Carl Bigham Sr. who had purchased it from the Wheeler family. The Wheelers' subsequent farm was at 1 Central Street next to the Ipswich River Park where Eddie Wheeler and his wife live today; Eddie Wheeler was born in the house at 193 Elm, according to Barry.

The summer of Barry's first year back, he decided to have a pumpkin patch for his nieces. The crop was so abundant in the fall that he sold a few from a cart in front of the carriage house. Regularly seeking the advice from farmers like Eddie Wheeler, Lyman Fancy and his grandfather, Barry expanded the stand's offerings to other vegetables in 1997.

"Anything I sell I grow myself or get from other local farms. It is all local produce." Customers enjoyed fresh corn, cukes, zucchini, apples, peaches, even hubbard squash. Blue hubbard was actually developed in Massachusetts years ago. Barry had heard that Eddie Wheeler's father was king of the blue hubbard squash, and controlled the market with squash he grew on the Elm Street farm.

As Barry continues to expand the business (he now has a location on Route 28), he will need more help. This past summer his sister, Bethany LeCaine, an Andover resident whose husband owns Pro Lanes Bowling on Main Street, helped at the Rowe Farm Stand.

"My sister was a very valuable worker," said Barry. "She is really good with customers. I would not have been able to run the stand without her." Bethany would bring her four- and seven-year-old daughters to help. Sometimes they even set up their own lemonade stand.

Bethany also lived with her grandfather for a time. In 1989 she came from California to spend the summer with Grandpa Rowe just after his second wife, Florence, had moved into a nursing home. Working at a bank here, she met her husband and stayed. A few years later she and her husband and small children lived with Granddad while saving for their first home.

"When I first moved back I helped Grandpa with the garden. He let me drive the tractor. He'd sit on the harrow to weigh it down. I always worried he'd fall off." One day Bethany and her granddad put the trailer on the back of the mower and drove up back to transport firewood. "He piled so much wood on the trailer that he had to ride standing up. When we got back to the farm I stopped too suddenly, and he went flying off the trailer! Landed in the grass upside down. But laughing. He scared me half to death. He was eighty years old at the time."

Well into his eighties Grandpa Rowe rode his bike every day. He stood on his head every morning and evening.

"You're laughing, but I've seen it!" recounted Barry.

Barry likes the rustic image the farm lends to his new business, such a contrast to the sterility of Los Angeles. "I see potential." The barn burned down in the 1950s, but the carriage house is filled with fifty years of old farm and horse equipment for plowing. Has Barry Grant tried to clean any of it out?

"My grandfather has plans for everything. Let me give you an example—the TWA boarding ladder."

After serving in the Navy, Dana Row Sr. was a mechanic for American Airlines, hired the third year it was in business. A real pioneer in the aeronautics business, he has worked on everything from the Ford Tri-motor to the 747.

The TWA boarding ladder had been left on American Airline's tarmac. Grandpa Rowe's boss tried unsuccessfully to get TWA to remove it. Finally he offered it to Rowe. The TWA boarding ladder came to Rowe Farm from Logan Airport towed behind Rowe's car. Imagine it coming up Route 1! Rowe has used it to pick apples, peaches, cherries and pears ever since.

Granddad Rowe built his own tractors from old car parts, sometimes using discarded airplane tires. He has a use for everything. "My farm stand signs," Barry pointed out, "are painted on crates Boeing used to ship airplane parts to Logan years ago. Some of the engine crates still have the packing slips in them. They are good wooden boxes."

Giving his full attention to the farm, Barry had to turn down comedy opportunities. The frost here, Barry will do some guest comedy spots and work his way back into that business. "I've tried a lot of things; everything evolves," he said, "but as long as Granddad is around, I'll be here."

—November 13, 1998

219 Park Street— Don and Sue Elliott's Restoration Project

Twenty-five years ago, Don and Sue Elliott bought the Federalistperiod home at 219 Park Street at the corner of Central Street from Margaret Murphy. "The house was one step from being condemned," remembers Don Elliott. "My brother, Ricky, went right through the hallway floor by the front door."

After propping up the house to replace forty feet of sill, matching intricate moldings and replacing period hardware, there is only one bedroom left to paper. But the Elliotts will put their restored treasure on the market in the spring, because last February they purchased the Field Hodges House near the North Andover Public Library, a home that has only had two other owners since 1839 and is in great need of repair. Its restoration is being supervised by the Society for the Preservation of New England Antiquities (SPNEA) that owns or oversees some sixty properties in New England.

SPNEA came to the Elliotts' Park Street home when they first bought it in 1975, providing an architectural history and survey of the home. SPNEA believed the chimney and beehive oven in the family room were part of an older home that dates back to the mid-1700s.

Barbara O'Brien, a member of the North Reading Historical Society who has devoted years to researching the history of North Reading homes, does not believe the back, or kitchen portion of the house necessarily stood on that property prior to construction of the 1801 structure.

"The back could have come from somewhere else," says Barbara. "You cannot assume there was an older house there. They moved buildings around in those days. They would just jack it up and roll it on trees, pulling it with oxen. The Second Meeting House was hauled up Elm Street this way," she says. In the eighteenth and nineteenth centuries, it was easier and less expensive to move buildings than to cut new wood; there was no problem disconnecting plumbing or electricity because there wasn't any, Barbara explains.

Don points out, however, that they did not generally move chimneys. SPNEA said that the tabby brick in the earliest of three fireplaces in the center chimney suggests the older portion of the house dates to the 1730s or 1740s, a time when this handmade (but not too durable) brick was used extensively.

From town records there is no disputing, however, that on December 18, 1801, Nathanial Upton sold one-third acre to Asa Hart for $100 and by 1812, Asa and his brother Joseph Hart had built the house you see today at 219 Park Street. The white farmhouse having been completed, Asa sold the house and property to his brother Joseph for $1,000.

Peter Flint bought the home at public auction after Joseph Hart's death in 1826, and sold it to his son Peter G. Flint two years later. The homestead then stayed in the Flint family for over seventy-five years, until 1903. During the twentieth century three generations of Spicers owned this property for almost as long as the Flints.

Leonard "Gig" Stevens remembers the Spicer boys well. At a young age, one of the five boys drowned in the pond behind the house on Central Street in which Gig Stevens currently resides; in a trunk in their attic the Elliotts discovered the clothing in which the boy had drowned along with the death certificate. Kenny Spicer, four at the time, was with his two-year-old brother on the day before Christmas 1936 when Dean fell through the pond ice. He is still not sure why no one was watching them. "We had a lot of freedom," he remembers from his home in Easton, Pennsylvania. "My grandfather was up near the stone wall. I never heard anyone wail with grief like he did. You don't forget that."

Spicer cows often grazed near this pond, but it was the pond to the right of 219 Park Street where neighborhood kids skated. It was likely there was artillery practice on the hill up behind this pond during the Revolutionary War. Don Elliott found three, five-pound cannon balls behind his house when excavating for his swimming pool.

In the 1930s Gig Stevens worked for Spicer's Dairy, officially Meadow View Farm. He drove the milk route that delivered small bottles of milk to children at Batchelder School.

Lowell Spicer, one of Kenny's younger brothers, remembers the milking and the deliveries, especially in winter. Says Lowell Spicer's daughter, Karen, who still lives in North Reading, "None of them wanted to be farmers and take care of animals in all kinds of weather. It was very hard work."

In addition to driving the milk route, Gig Stevens also "drove" or herded the cows up Central Street to the pastures behind what is now Aldersgate Church. Peter Flint, brother of Charles, acquired land so that the grazing pastures extended all the way from Route 62 to North Street; he owned 100 acres. Over the years cows also grazed in the meadow on the south side of Park Street near the Ipswich River. The twentieth century Spicer farm ended at the stonewall where the high school cross-country team cuts through the woods.

In the early 1900s there were many dairies in North Reading. "The Wheelers had cows up on Elm," recalls Gig Stevens. "I worked for them on weekends for a dollar a day." Gig also recalls the Chaltz Dairy Farm on the left before the Thompson Country Club and Eisenhaure Dairy on Haverhill Street.

Kenny Spicer recalls his grandfather had thirty-five cows in a barn that sat close to Central Street right behind the garages of 219 Park. In those same garages still standing behind the Elliott's home, Spicer's Dairy bottled the milk.

"After the government required it, we took the milk up to Shawsheen Village (Andover) for pasteurization. United Farmers' Association. Took it up in twenty-five gallon cans, and then we'd bring it back to bottle, Spicer stoppers on the top," remembers Gig.

The dairy closed in 1948 or 1949 according to Kenny Spicer, but the ice cream stand next to 219 Park Street operated for at least a year after the untimely death in 1951 of his father Ralph Spicer at age forty-one.

"I was only eleven when we opened the ice cream stand," remembers Lowell Spicer.

"One time I got caught for working too late by some child welfare people. They wanted to know how old I was."

In addition to running the dairy, Ralph Spicer played trombone in the U. S. Coast Guard Auxiliary Band (the Elliotts have parade pictures from the attic), and was a captain in North Reading's Fire Department. As a private contractor he drove his own Diamond T school bus locally, and had strawberry fields he leased at the corner of Haverhill and Chestnut streets.

Al Rodgers, a local carpenter who specializes in restoration and replicated the "eyebrow window" in the Third Meeting House (Building on the Common) to replace the one that had rotted out, for years has worked with Don Elliott on the restoration of 219 Park Street. Al Rodgers remembers picking strawberries for Ralph Spicer. "I was young—fourteen or something. He paid me five cents per box."

Al fashioned all the doors in the Elliotts' house to match the one they found in the attic. "I can match any molding," he says. "It is nice to restore and bring back the old look. Lots of satisfaction in building things."

Don and Sue Elliott feel that same satisfaction. Don learned to love restoration from his late grandfather, Arthur Silvestro, a millwright and cabinetmaker who worked on the Park Street house with his grandson until he was ninety-six.

The whole family helping, Don's father, Dick, played a part in the acquisition of 219 Park Street. A Realtor in Stoneham at the time this property came on the market, Dick knew Margaret Murphy, the previous owner, and was able to inform his son and daughter-in-law about its availability early on.

With the flexibility of a real estate career, Dick has also pursued his love of acting. Today he is officially Ben Franklin for the city of

Boston, but he also has appeared in twenty-two episodes of "Spenser for Hire," two episodes of "Miami Vice" and several movies.

Dick and his wife, Muriel, arrive dressed as Mr. and Mrs. Ben Franklin as we are finishing this interview. In costume they visually take us back 200 years as they pose in front of the beehive oven where Don smokes his Thanksgiving turkey and their son, Jason, regularly makes brick oven pizza.

The Elliotts are pleased that their two children have taken such an interest in their passion for restoration. "Look at the kids," says Sue. "They love old things. They appreciate old things. They can restore old furniture. Rachel can wallpaper and stencil. Jason has completely rebuilt a 1970 Porsche 911."

Do the Elliotts have any advice for young couples thinking of buying the handyman special? "Know that it will take you twice as much money and twice as much time as you thought, to do it right," says Don.

Having lived for a year in one partitioned parlor room when Jason was still in a crib, Sue's advice is, "Don't try to live in it while you plaster."

—*January 5, 2001*

Two

When the Trolley Went to Martins Pond

Flint Memorial Hall, 1875

Dick and Dave Ham, Batchelder School Students in the 1940s

Richard Ham and his brother Dave thought it was quite an adventure to have baths in a galvanized tub in the kitchen and to visit the privy at the end of the shed when, in 1940, their family moved to 126 Chestnut Street, North Reading, a house with no central heat and no plumbing.

For six years their parents, Priscilla and Robert, rented the Elija Parker Jr. house for twenty-five dollars a month at which time they bought this charming 1799 colonial. Once they owned the property, the Hams replaced the coal and the kerosene stoves and installed indoor plumbing.

On September 1, 1940, Dick Ham started fifth grade at the Batchelder School. Younger brother David Ham began first grade the next fall, his class meeting in the adjacent Campbell House.

Originally built as the Healy Tavern, it was unable to compete with the Damon Tavern, and so the Campbell family bought the building that was to bear their name. Eventually the town acquired the Campbell house and used it to alleviate overcrowding in the town's only school. In 1950 the shoe box-shaped addition solved that problem, and the Campbell House was subsequently torn down.

"We still call it the new addition," volunteers Barbara, wife of Dave, who grew up in North Reading on Gordon Road when the town's population was just under 3,000. Barbara remembers a talent night with a tumbling match in the cafeteria during the spring of 1950, but the classroom space in the new addition was not available until the fall.

"We never had a cafeteria before the addition," she recalls. "Dave and Dick delivered the glass milk bottles and chips, which C. W. Spears Dairy supplied, and everyone ate at their desk."

"I thought I was pretty important delivering the milk," remembers Dick.

"Those jobs went to responsible eighth- and ninth-graders," adds Dave.

When Dick was in elementary school, Ralph Sturke was both superintendent of schools and principal. Four private bus contractors picked up students from Liberty Acres, Looney Hill, Holts Grove, The Pond and The Center, as locals referred to the various areas of town. Hailing from Liberty Acres, Barbara rode on Ralph Spicer's bus. The Ham brothers traveled to school on Artie Jeanes' bus and waited at the corner of Haverhill and Chestnut.

Dave recalls one unusual October morning at the bus stop. As part of the war effort, the Miller family on the corner were raising a steer to have slaughtered. On this particular morning, the steer got loose and crossed Haverhill Street. As Emma Downs watched out her back door, horrified, the animal chased young Dave to Mrs. Collins Putnam's back door where Mrs. Putnam let the terrified Dave Ham into the kitchen of her saltbox house.

"I wasn't the speediest thing afoot," admits Dave. "There was steer saliva on the back of my pants. But Mom said I never let go of my lunch box. I didn't want to drop the black thermos bottle. Hard to say if I feared the steer or the broken thermos more."

Dick, whose teaching career spanned forty some years, in his tenth year of retirement still regularly substitutes at Reading High School. He has fond memories of favorite teachers at Batchelder School where his education began. Ninth-grade science teacher Mildred Barmby, upper level English teacher Barbara Bacon, and physical education teacher Frances Murphy come to mind. Barbara Ham remembers Mrs. Barmby teaching her students to name the clouds: nimbus, cirrus, cumulus. There were no science labs or hands-on experiments. Once a week, the music teacher, Miss Vera Roche, came to class with her singing book. "Week after week we learned 'do, re, mi, fa, so' as she beat that book with her pitch pipe," says Dick.

Barbara also recalls that Coach Murphy introduced a gymnastics program for girls when the athletic program was ninety percent for the boys. The Batchelder School gym also served another purpose—the place for school dances and record hops. To be prepared for such social occasions, the Ham boys both took ballroom dancing classes: Dave, from Eddie Conron, son of the town's switchboard operator Flossie, and Dick, in the Reading studio of Barbara Monroe whose husband owned Monroe Fuel.

Dave remembers his first official date with his wife, Barbara Long. It was October of ninth grade when Harry Stokes and his orchestra, consisting of Harry and his wife, on piano and drums respectively, played tunes like "Slow Boat to China" at a dance in the Third Meeting House. "My dad and I picked Barbara up across town in the green 1941 Ford. The dance was probably over at nine."

Set up in the Batchelder School hallway was a plywood booth from which a responsible student sold stamps for war bonds. Barbara was often that student. Children pasted the stamps in a little booklet. When they had collected $18.75 worth of stamps they turned them in for a twenty-five dollar war bond. "Barbara sold them. I bought them. It was a very patriotic feeling to buy those stamps and a little chance to flirt," recalls Dave.

During the war, both Ham brothers remember rationing sugar and saving tinfoil. "Use it up, wear it out, make it do, or do without!" was the wartime slogan every child knew. Soles of shoes were made of a synthetic rubber so the real rubber could go to the war effort. Victory bikes had no chrome on them.

"Those bikes were made with terrible, cheap metal. I was glad I got my bike before the war started," says Dick. "But people did not begrudge it. When my father listened to Lowell Thomas on the radio news every night, there was total silence in the house." Dick admits that most of his understanding of the war came from the black and white pictures in the *Life* magazines at Ted Crosby's barbershop on Dutton's Corner. Both boys would ride there on their bikes to get a twenty-five-cent hair cut.

In the 1940s the closest movie theater was in Reading square. For twelve cents you could see Abbott and Costello, but you had to pay twenty cents to ride Lane's bus. Herbie Mosher drove Lane's bus, and was well acquainted with the habits of his riders. He made a continuous loop from North Reading center in front of the Flint Memorial building to the Reading train station. Kitty's restaurant was one of the stops.

"Kitty's was a tiny dive," remarks Barbara. "We weren't allowed to go into Kitty's."

Once school let out for the summer, what would the Ham brothers do to entertain themselves long before the days of Nintendo and Little League?

"We did our own thing. Invented our own games, played in Mentus' woods," says Dave. With his best friends—Donny Upton, Wendell McIntire, and the Thorp boys on New Street—Dave devised war games. A hollowed out, fallen tree on the hill behind his house became their submarine.

Across the street at 124 Chestnut there was a small Cities Service gas station. Harold Chase had installed a pump to create a job for his son Kenny, who had a chronic kidney condition. A generous man, Harold would provide Dave and his pals with bits and pieces of old machinery. "We'd haul it up into the tree to outfit our submarine with periscopes and radar." Harold also had a grease pit. The two cement pads for the car tires are still an obvious part of the flower bed next to the barn. The gas station had an electric wire; its bell let the Chases know when a customer drove up for gas.

William Mentus was another neighbor who welcomed kids as he went about his daily activities, tending to his dairy farm on Cedar Street. "We'd help him herd the cows back to the barn, or he'd let us pitch hay on to the wagon," Dave volunteers.

"I thought it was quite a privilege to watch Mr. Mentus milk a cow," says Dick. "It was nice to hear the cow bells." William, however, was what Dick describes as "casual" with his cows. One night the herd got loose and woke the neighborhood as they circled the Cities Service gas pump, stepping repeatedly on the electric wire that rang the bell!

Joleen Ham, Dick's wife and a self-proclaimed city girl from Portland, Maine, remembers her first visit to North Reading in 1951. The sounds of cow bells and roosters made her suspect she had come to the end of the earth to visit this Bowdoin College student with whom she had fallen in love.

While they were still in grade school, Dick and his friends Stillman "Stump" Putnam, Robert Upton, and Floyd Downs spent much of their summer on their bicycles. There were four variety stores in town: Molly's, better known today as Ryer's store; Sadie Witcomb's in the Weeks building; Winnie Galvin's at the foot of Oakdale Road; and Dud Wilson's, which was at the corner of Washington Street and Park Street East.

"We'd make the rounds," recalls Dick. "When it got dull, we'd make a picnic and take a ride to the Stoneham Zoo." If they needed caps for Fourth of July cap pistols, Sadie's was the only place you could get them. She had candy, too, but they did not buy it. "We suspected it was prewar candy sold post war."

Sometimes the boys were given important errands on their bikes. It was Dick's responsibility to ride to Flossie Conron's house to pay the phone bill for his mother. He did not mind this assignment because he got to watch Flossie connect the wires that allowed neighbors to call one another. "One time I was watching her work, and number 349 lit up. That was our phone number!"

"There's a fire over there on Cedar Street," Dick heard one of Flossie's operators tell Flossie's husband Harold, who was the fire chief and the paid fire department in its entirety.

"What's happened?" exclaimed Dick. He got on his bike and went screaming back to his house to find the field behind his home on fire. Dave and his accomplice, Freddy Thorp, had set the dry field ablaze, lighting a little fire they were sure they could put out.

"I got a swipe at me with a broom as I ran through the kitchen and right up the stairs to bed," recalls Dave. "Later I got a serious lecture from Harold Conron."

Seldom in an adversarial role with any town authority, the fire incident notwithstanding, Dave fondly remembers the summer treat of watching the first black and white TV in town, which was situated in the upstairs of the old firehouse. "We'd go over to watch the Red Sox games. All the kids were welcome. There was a Coke machine and couches up there. The firemen's auxiliary kept it nice."

As they became teens, the Ham brothers had summer jobs in North Reading. Both remember painting fire hydrants for the department of public works. Dick worked in the drive-in movie theater where Stop and Shop is now. In 1950, on the opening night of the Star-lite, he parked cars with a flashlight. He also worked the refreshment stand frying potatoes. "Cleaning those fryers was an awful job," says Dick.

Barbara was a hostess several summers at Sailor Tom's, an elaborate eatery on Main Street with a trout pool from which customers could catch their own dinner. There was a little zoo with peacocks and a PT boat gift shop next to what is now Wingate nursing home. The only reminder of that popular seafood place that closed its doors in the late 1950s is a beached ship on Franklin Street that Sailor Tom had designed and built for his home.

The Hams both worked a few summers at G. H. Atkinson's, a grocery store on Haven Street in Reading. With a different style from today's supermarket, customers would come to the counter and make their requests for soup or tuna. Then young people like Dick or Dave would run to the shelves or push the ladder over to retrieve the requested items. For twenty-five dollars per week, the Hams also drove the store's delivery truck. On-line shopping has nothing on this older system. In fact, many items were regularly delivered to homes in the 1940s. The Ham's neighbor, Collins Putman, drove a laundry delivery truck, and Jack Ellis delivered fish in North Reading. All of this was accomplished without street numbers on houses.

Their father was on the planning board, so Dick and Dave got the job of measuring streets and numbering houses one summer. Armed with a tape measure, graph paper and penny postcards, the Ham brothers measured one hundred foot lengths, assigning numbers to the intervals whether a house was there or not. If there was a house, they sent a postcard to its owner giving the newly assigned street number. Dave measured and numbered Main and Elm, while Dick did the same for Chestnut and Mt. Vernon streets. It was a hot job so after work they might go to "Drinkies" (the Drinkwater property, now Ipswich River Park) for a swim in the Ipswich River.

Both still live in town on the very streets they numbered. "We have good memories. That's probably why we stayed around so long," says Dick.

—*May 1, 2001*

Pat and Veronica Lee, the Horseshoe Café

Owned by the same family for seventy-two years, the Horseshoe Café originally sold freshly pressed apple cider and hot dogs to city folks who might come on the trolley for a day's outing at Martins Pond. D. P. Murphy owned the establishment in the 1920s during prohibition. Through its history, the Horseshoe has also been called a club and a lounge.

When prohibition ended in 1935, D. P. Murphy sold the Horseshoe Club to his brother-in-law, John Twomey, who had recently come to this country from County Kerry, Ireland. The business didn't change hands again until 1955 when Patrick and Veronica Lee bought the Horseshoe from Veronica's Uncle John.

"We lived in Woodside, New York, at the time," remembers Veronica. "Uncle John called us up. 'I'm going to sell, and I want to give you the first bid.'" Veronica remembers sitting in their Chevy under the Horseshoe sign and asking her uncle, "How much of this is yours?"

"Anything you see would be yours," he answered. She wanted to see the inside of the attached house where she and her husband Pat and eleven-month-old Pat Jr., who now owns the café, would be living, but there were tenants. "A house is a house, girl," he said.

"My uncle thought the sun, moon and stars set on my husband," said Veronica.

"But he charged me for the place, dear," jokes Pat Lee Sr. "He and I got along well." John Twomey stayed around and worked four hours a day at the Shoe until he died in 1958. It was a smooth transition, no grand opening. Some people did not even know the establishment had changed hands in 1955 when Pat and Veronica Lee bought it for $35,000.

And why had Uncle John offered his niece and her husband first chance to buy his business in North Reading? In the early 1950s, when the couple was living in New York City, and Pat was driving a bus for the New York Transit Authority, Veronica's uncle John returned from a trip to Ireland by steamship in the midst of a dock strike. With several trunks, and his own children unable to rescue him from the dock, Uncle John was grateful that Pat took a day off to help him and his wife get themselves and their baggage home. Uncle John never forgot the kindness. "See what an act of charity did?" remarked Veronica.

Pat and Veronica left Ireland on the very same day in April 1948, one by boat and the other by plane, and although they had lived their first twenty years only seventeen miles apart in County Cavan and County Kerry, they never met in Ireland.

"We heard about the gold on the streets of America," said Pat. "They gave me a broom to sweep up the gold, but I never saw any of it." Two years after the couple met at a house party on Long Island, Pat and Veronica were wed at Sacred Heart Church in Jackson Heights, Long Island.

Farmers in County Kerry and County Caven, the Lee and Twomey families never owned pubs in Ireland. When the Lees became owners of the Horseshoe they introduced an Irish pub atmosphere, serving snacks like hot dogs, quahogs, individual-sized pizzas and sandwiches. The melted ham and cheese sandwich was legendary. When their son Pat bought the Shoe in 1985, he adopted a southwestern theme, familiar to him from the three years he worked in Texas. Because full liquor licenses were based on the population of the town, in the early days, it was easier at first to obtain a "club" license to sell liquor. The Shoe issued membership cards and even had a board of directors as required by Massachusetts state law.

"Regular customers would give me a ten; I'd give them two fives back, and they'd be a member," recalls Pat Lee Sr.

The law also required the town to vote every two years whether it would be "wet" or "dry."

"We had to wait up to see how the vote went each election day, and whether we could open our doors for business in the morning," said Veronica.

The Lees, in the tradition of Uncle John, who often took money to the fire station and asked it be distributed to needy families anonymously, have supported a number of charities over the years. Beginning in 1955, Horseshoe Lounge raised money for the Jimmy Fund with softball games, road races, raffles and golf tournaments.

Their efforts have amounted to over $350,000 donated to cancer research in children. Last fall the Horseshoe Café had patrons bring canned goods to restock the North Reading Food Pantry on Thanksgiving eve, one of their busiest evenings. The Horseshoe's celebration of the North Reading/Lynnfield football rivalry on Thanksgiving easily lasts twenty-four hours at the Shoe, including breakfast before the game.

"St. Patrick's Day is also huge for us," said Pat Jr. For years Mary Richard's Step Dancing Studio, where Pat and Veronica's daughter Kathleen studied Irish dancing, provided at least three age groups of step dancers for March 17 at the Shoe. Today the step-dancing tradition continues with Rita O'Shea's school in Lawrence providing the performers.

"St. Patrick's Day in Ireland is not a party," said Veronica. "It is a religious holiday there. Pubs are closed. No parades. Everyone attends mass in the morning. It is a family day."

Preparing for holidays at the Horseshoe was always a family project. Young Pat remembers helping to make hundreds of sandwiches at Christmas time. Veronica loved decorating the hall that holds 125 since it was rebuilt in 1961.

"The first week in December the two of us would come back after closing at eleven to put up the Christmas decorations. We loved to do it. We'd be up to five in the morning." Father Lane came in once while holiday preparations were under way.

"You should be outside of heaven, waiting to step in," he remarked on how hard the Lees were working.

"If you counted the hours my husband worked, you'd be more tired than you thought you were," said Veronica.

—October 1, 1999

Lee and Beth Caplan, Abbott Shoe

Back to school. Time to buy the new Skechers, the Adidas, the Steve Madden platform shoes. Abbott Shoe on Main Street is a busy place. Pat Jones will give you a number at the cash register as she has for eighteen years, and if you need to wait more than a minute on the carpeted boxes, you can read *Zoo Babies* or *The Little Engine That Could.*

"We run a local family business with a reputation for discount. Abbott Shoe has been taking care of kids, moms and dads for generations," says Lee Caplan, manager of Abbott Shoe for twenty-one years.

"She's a nine shoe, a ten sneaker. Do you want to try on the blue?" asks Ainsley Hollinger, one of three workers in a black vest and jeans.

"These run a little big—maybe next year for the clogs," says Eileen Russo, employed since 1983. On the recommendation of her friend Nancy Stewart, Eileen came in on a Friday at the end of August and started fitting shoes the following Monday.

"We went on a merry-go-round, and a dragon coaster, and on the really fast turn it goes *shrissh,"* explains Rachel, a three-year-old customer in a pink dress trying on clogs that have little mirrors for trim.

"I would have to close my eyes if I went on a dragon coaster. Here, let's take a walk in these shoes," suggests Beth Caplan, wife of the manager and a nursery school teacher at Temple Emmanuel, Andover, during the school year. "I come in here to play during the summer," she says with a smile.

"You have to like kids to work here," volunteers Eileen.

Past the cash register and across from the adult sneaker display is a framed picture of the Abbott Shoe Company, its four-story wooden structure having once been located on the Ipswich River where the North Reading Shopping Center stands today. Built in 1855 by Samuel Abbott, it occupied a site, according to town historian Pat Romeo, in the vicinity of an early gristmill that ground grain before the 1800s, a lumber mill in the early 1800s, and the Otis P. Symonds Box Factory in the 1870s.

Samuel Abbott, the grandson of the man who built Abbott Shoe Factory, married a woman named Clarissa. Although she had lived in town since the early 1950s, her husband once said, "If you're not born here, you're a foreigner."

"Well, he never was anything but a foreigner in Portland, Maine," comments Clarissa.

Ken Jones, a North Reading native, remembers, "A lady died here at ninety-two, having moved to North Reading at six months of age, and obituary read 'although not a native ...' "

Ken's first memories of Abbott Shoe were related to his father's trucking business. Daily, at age six, he was riding with his uncle Jack from the Abbott Factory to Rowes Wharf in Boston to deliver Easifit slippers.

"My uncle took the shoe haul every morning by 8:30. We'd pick up twenty or thirty huge cases of shoes. Wouldn't drive if it was raining because they were open trucks—had to double up the next day." By age fourteen Ken was backing up trucks in the lot and had learned to grease them.

"At one time my dad had seventy-five trucks in the yard," he says. World War II, however, took most of the drivers overseas, and the Jones brothers went into retail, building the first strip mall in North Reading, the building which today houses the Hornet's Nest Sub Shop and Video Outpost.

It was in 1917 at the outbreak of World War I that Marion Thompson moved to North Reading, her father having come a year earlier to work for George Wright and Mr. Whurley, partners who had bought out Samuel Abbott. Marion was only six years old, but she remembers that Wright and Whurley envisioned a signature hand-turned men's slipper made by soaking and stretching the leather until it was pliable, then stretching and pulling it onto a molded form by employing a hot iron.

As the years went by the company introduced a women's comfort shoe, and Marion worked as a high school student in the finishing room, buffing out smudges on the leather. Another summer she made tags for the shoe racks.

Eileen Russo also worked at the factory, beginning when she was fifteen. "Mel Ross taught me how to run the leather punch. It was a big machine, but I liked it because it was near the window. The smell of the glue was just terrible," she says.

Alice Tarbox Nickerson's father went to work at the Abbott Shoe factory when she was only ten years old. "My mother worked there for a week, but it was not her cup of tea," says Alice. She also worked briefly in the factory, but she worked far longer as a North Reading telephone operator in Flossie and Harold Conron's front parlor on Park Street West.

"There were 500 phones in town when they switched over to dial, sometimes as many as eight on a party line," she says.

Marion's father also changed jobs, leaving the shoe factory to become North Reading's postmaster in the early 1940s when the post office was in the Jones Brother's grocery store. Subbing for ailing RFD driver William Hayward, Marion delivered the mail for her dad one Christmas week. "I never worked in such a mess. Up at Martins Pond there would be ten to twelve boxes on a post, not one with a name on it. Of course if the mail got in the wrong box everyone knew whom it belonged to," she says.

From Wright and Whurley, the Abbott Shoe Company passed to a Mr. Ridgefield in 1926, manufacturing shoes until shortly after World War II, according to the framed picture in the store. In 1957, the factory reopened as Ross Shoe Company, brothers Howard and Melvin Ross having outgrown their small facility in Lynn.

Soon Mel Ross was running an outlet shoe business on the first floor of the factory.

"Mel was used to wheeling and dealing job lots," said Lee Caplan, Mel's son-in-law and Abbott Shoe manager. "Today I have one hundred styles for back-to-school shoes. On the other hand, Mel would buy a 3,000 pair lot. Back-to-school season then had only one style."

At first in the hotel business in New York City, Lee changed careers partly to cut back on business travel and the stress of city life. Managing his wife's family shoe store seemed very natural since his family had also been in the shoe business. Lee's father, Jack, who works part time at the North Reading store, retired from the shoe business he managed in Worcester for forty-five years.

"When I started here ninety percent of footwear came from manufacturers who are now out of business. There was a shoe district in Boston on Lincoln Street. There had to be hundreds of small jobbers. Mel and I would go in at 8:00 A.M. to pick out shoes."

Lee is grateful for having learned that aspect of the business by watching Mel. Today, however, there is no shoe district on Lincoln Street and no jobbers—not one. Typically shoes are made in China, and the seconds are discarded, never making it to outlets in the United States.

After the fire at the Abbott Shoe factory in the 1960s, Mel Ross' shoe store moved to Bow Street where the post office had been, and where Beth Kamhi's chiropractic practice and the *Transcript* offices are today. By then the shoe factory portion of the business had moved to Puerto Rico.

My father-in-law from Maine often told the story of finding a single shoe he liked in the store window at that dusty Bow Street location. "Wait just a minute," Mel would say, cheerfully heading for a cardboard barrel at the rear of the store and digging through the bin to find the mate. It was a common occurrence.

Abbott Shoe relocated in 1979 to Washington Street. In 1988, the business moved again, this time to the Atlantic (now Star) Shopping Plaza. Finally, just three years ago this October, the Abbott Shoe Store, still under the same management, moved to its present location where the rectory for Saint Theresa's stood years ago.

Every September Abbott Shoe sells one to two hundred pairs of kids' shoes each day. "We sometimes go through the numbers twice," said Eileen Russo. Patent leather Mary Janes, Keds, boots, Nike sneakers. Lee Caplan, his wife, his son, two full-time and ten part-time workers will measure children's feet and ask them to take a walk down to the foot mirrors to see how they look.

—*September 1, 2000*

Patricia Romeo, Organist and Auxiliary Policewoman

The Los Angeles Police Department's motto is to protect and serve. Pat Romeo contends that police work is not really unlike church work—to work in either, one must want to help people. Pat balances two careers. The first woman to serve as an armed uniformed patrol back-up for the North Reading police force, she also has sung for the pope and played the organ at the Vatican. She is music director and organist for St. Patrick's Church in Lawrence.

While Pat's Italian grandfather and Irish grandmother made their first home in the North End, by the time Pat was born the extended family was living on a chicken farm in rural Revere. "Lots of people during the Depression had little businesses on the side. They would deliver eggs, sell chickens, live or dressed," she said.

Her grandfather, Alexander Clark, having attended University of Mass Amherst Agricultural School, often experimented with different types of feed for his poultry, and kept the barn warm all winter so the hens would continue to lay eggs during the cold months.

In her teen years Pat loved to ride horses. "Sarge, the best horse I ever rode, was retired from the United States Cavalry; I often rode in Melrose around Spot Pond." While living in this idyllic rural environment, Pat also remembers being frightened by precautionary wartime practices. "I remember the blackout shades, the car headlights painted half black, the newspapers with the box of arrows in the upper right-hand corner that detailed the progress of troops in Europe." As little children, "we knew it was something about life and death," she said. Grandfather's garden, however, was not just a wartime Victory Garden. Tom Spinelli hoed and planted well into his eighties. "As he lay dying he worried about weeding the tomatoes," said Pat.

At age fifteen, Pat had a job singing for the Baptist Church in Revere. Her mother's side Protestant, Pat attended the Methodist church in Revere as a child. Because her charismatic choral director at Revere High School, William Goss, belonged to the Baptist Church, she became a member of his choir in her late teens. "All my girl friends, however, were Catholic; I often went to mass with them."

When Pat was a high school senior, the Revere High School chorus won many competitions, leading to an opportunity to sing with the Boston Pops in June 1954 and Pat sang a solo. "We sang Victor Herbert selections. My solo was the 'Italian Street Song'—something like that." It was on that evening that Frank Romeo, a young man who worked for Pat's uncle, first laid eyes on his future wife.

Pat went on to study music at Boston University where she met lifelong friend, Nancy Henry Ferretti, also a student there. "We were so lucky. So many opportunities. We sang the United States premier performance of Carl Orff's *Carmina Burana* under guest conductor Leopold Stokowski. "I still know every word of it," she said. It was during these college years that Pat converted to Catholicism.

In the late 1950s Revere and Everett were becoming more urban. Pat and Frank looked at property in North Reading, where her grandparents had summered in a cottage on Martins Pond long ago. The Romeos bought their present home on Haverhill Street in 1961. "Monsignor John Lane came to visit us the first week we were here and asked me to help with the choir at St. Theresa's."

With five children born in six years, Romeo had little time for a job. After a year or two, however, she did become director of the St. Theresa's choirs, sharing the organ position with Joe Pothier.

A desperate call from St. Thomas Parish in Wilmington to substitute at mass for an organist, who had died midweek, subsequently led to a four-year position there. After her children had completed their schooling in North Reading, and after she had supported them in Little League, Girl Scouts and volunteer work at the Hood Elementary School, Pat had time to become the organist at Immaculate Conception Church in Everett Square. "It was a busy church. I loved it. But I always worried about being late for a funeral if I was stuck in traffic on Route 1."

When Pope Paul VI came to Boston in 1979, Pat was soloist for a 300-voice archdiocesean papal choir on Boston Common. After the event was over the choir auditioned down to fifty voices. This smaller choir traveled to Rome in May 1985 for the elevation of Bernard Law to cardinal.

While in Rome, Pat played for mass at St. Paul's, St. Maria Maggiore, St. John Lateran, and at St. Peter's itself. "I had fifteen minutes to try the five manual organ in St. Peter's before the mass, and every stop had Italian printed on it." Still actively involved with music for the Boston Archdiocese, Pat schedules all the musicians for the daily mass on Boston cable TV.

For the last ten years, Pat has been the organist and choir director at St. Patrick's Church in Lawrence. St. Patrick's being as busy a church as the one in Everett, she typically plays three weekend masses. On St. Patrick's Day she will play a special mass at 10:30 A.M. Initiated by Pat, the March 17 mass features a children's choir, violin and vocal soloists, and a prelude of early Irish traditional O'Carolan music from the eighteenth century.

Although her two careers seldom intersect, six years ago and for several years following, Pat has sung for the Boston Archdiocese's annual Law Enforcement Mass dressed in her North Reading police uniform. Cardinal Bernard Law officiates.

How did she become Officer Romeo? Police Chief Gordon Berridge had served with Pat on the Bicentennial Commission from 1974–76. The bicentennial celebrations over, Pat was looking for other ways to serve locally. She responded to a notice in the local paper seeking volunteer auxiliary police.

"When I asked for the application, Gordon tried to discourage me. 'You'll have to carry a gun and learn to shoot straight,' he said." With the exception of her great uncle Edward Forsythe's being a policemen in Dublin, Ireland, no one else in Pat's family was in law enforcement. When she joined North Reading's Auxiliary Police in 1976, however, and later the Special Police Force, Pat's husband, Frank, joined with her.

While there was a bit of negative backlash from some of the older officers towards women joining the force, Pat successfully completed her six months of evening training at the North East Regional Police Institute. Over the years, the department had often enlisted the services of women to help with female prisoners in the jail. In 1972, Marilyn Reynolds was the first police "matron" to be appointed crossing guard.

"I don't think they took us seriously," said Marilyn. "But we knew enough to take what was said with a grain of salt. They made our lives a little miserable, but that was not unusual (for women) in the day," she said. Marilyn's primary assignments were at the corner of Park and Elm streets and on Southwick Road near the Little Elementary School. There are children she "crossed" who are on the police force today.

As Officer Romeo, Pat worked shifts, had road detail, got called for block dances and the Memorial Day parade. Both women still assist occasionally with female arrests, traffic control, and transport of female prisoners.

"We have to qualify with weapons every year," explained Pat. "Today we use semiautomatic 9mm Glocks, replacing the .38-caliber police special revolvers we used to carry."

Two of Pat and Frank's five children have become police officers. Detective Thomas Romeo is currently lead detective for the North Reading force. Corporal Daniel Romeo has worn the blue uniform on the LAPD for ten years.

"I did not encourage my boys to go into police work. It can be hugely stressful. You know when you put on the uniform and the badge you are saying, 'I'm willing to risk my life for every person in this town.' " For Pat, the most satisfying part of police work is in seeing the positive result when she has talked to a young person in crisis. The most discouraging part of the job is seeing people ruin their lives with drugs and alcohol.

Since the early 1970s Pat has observed dramatic changes in police work, both locally and nationally. Typewriters, telephones and teletype have been replaced by computers, making access to information available in an instant from the other side of the country. DNA testing has maximized accuracy in identification. Pat credits the late Gordon Berridge (chief from 1967–1983) with bringing the department to a new level of sophistication by encouraging and facilitating education of police officers.

Prior to the incorporation of the town in 1853, law enforcement was the responsibility of constables who posted legal notices, served papers and kept the peace. Two constables served the town at the time of its incorporation with a combined salary of $21.75, according to records Pat compiled for the police department. It was not until 1912 that there was any mention of a police department in town reports; John Hume served as the first North Reading chief.

Tom Croswell, father of Ellsworth Croswell who owned the funeral home across from the library, became police chief in 1921, holding that position until 1949. In 1937 town reports show that overcoats were stolen from the Grange Hall on April 27. The coats having been recovered, Cambridge Courthouse sentenced the thief to four or five years in state prison. Under Chief Croswell, police took the town census door to door. Tom Croswell personally delivered the Town Report to every home. He knew his constituency.

Gordon Berridge joined the force in 1955 while E. Hudson "Hud" Rodgers was police chief. In 1959, with 201 arrests in the town, Chief Rodgers included "A Prayer for Modern Parents" in his annual report to the town. Upon Chief Berridge's retirement in 1983, Lieutenant Henry Purnell became North Reading's chief of police.

In her varied service to the town, Pat has been a longtime member of the Historical Society, the Historical Commission, and the Historic District Commission. Town residents have elected her three times to the Community Planning Commission for which she is running a fourth time this spring. At one time she was even assistant dog officer. Loving the town's history and wanting to pass it on to the next generation, Pat has promoted the opening of the Putnam House to school groups, especially fourth-graders. On these occasions she explains how early settlers baked bread in the large colonial fireplace and carded wool. "I sometimes cook squash soup in the fireplace," she said. Pat occasionally is recognized in the grocery store. A school child once passed her in three different aisles before tugging on her mother's sleeve, "Mom, it's true, it is Mrs. Putnam!"

—*March 3, 2000*

Barbara O'Brien, Town Historian

In 1949 when Barbara Aylward O'Brien was in the fifth grade at the Batchelder School, her class took a history tour of the North Reading town center. She remembers her teacher standing in front of the Third Meeting House on the Common and explaining that it used to be a church. In her mind that building on the Common was somehow associated with the Union Congregational Church across the street to which her family belonged, but she could not quite figure it out. "It bothered me for years," said Barbara.

Fifty years later, she is working on a book on the history of North Reading, which she intends to complete in time for the town's 150th birthday in 2003. In order to give herself sufficient time to proceed with her research and her writing, Barbara recently decided to resign from the Historical Commission on which she had served since the mid-1970s.

"I will still be restoration director of the Putnam House for the Historical Society. In fact, I will be able to devote more time to that.

The Putnam House needs a new roof." She will also have time to devote to working with the Minitmen to rebuild the Elm Street District school house privy and the shoe shop, which DPW supervisor Fran Pothier discovered at the far west side of the Riverside Cemetery last fall. The district schools were closed in 1917 when Batchelder School opened; these disintegrating sheds have been used for storage at the cemetery for eighty-two years. Barbara will also continue to serve as a trustee of North Reading trust funds, a job she has held since 1979.

Barbara moved to North Reading in 1946. Her father just out of the service, her parents were out for a Sunday drive when they came across a new housing development on Damon Street. With the GI Bill offering low interest loans of two to three percent, her father, James, decided to purchase this $10,000 home in the country.

For the first year, with no one her age on the street, Barbara rode her bike from her house to Park Street West to play with her Batchelder school friends.

"I regret that children today do not know the safety of riding a bike alone, or being comfortable taking rides from people who offer," she said.

In the other direction she could ride to the Ipswich River bridge to swim in the "mud hole," sometimes without seeing a single car on Route 62 the whole way. The river had a beach with the finest white sand, and an enormous tree with a rope swing that the boys used for jumping.

Everything changed her second year in North Reading when a child her age, with the most gorgeous red hair, moved from Wilmington into the house on the corner of Damon and Park streets, beginning what was to be a lifelong friendship. "It was just wonderful having Nancy Henry (Ferretti) on my street. She won all the freckle contests. Freckle contests were big in those days."

Flossie Conron had the town's telephone switchboard in her parlor two houses to the right of Jones Brothers' Hardware. "My family had a phone with a crank on it," she said.

Vera and Jimmy Skinner owned Skinner's Cab, and if Vera did not answer your call, Flossie could tell you that Vera had gone to Reading to pick someone up at the depot. Hudson E. Rodgers was the police chief and the entire police force all by himself. "Hud took care of everybody. He was conscious of people's reputations and never let stories out," recalled Barbara. Back then, Ralph Douglas collected the trash in his pickup truck if you did not want to haul it to the dump yourself.

Barbara's last year at the Batchelder School was the first year of the building's "shoe-box extension," the wing that runs north and south. Most of the forty-eight students that graduated in 1950 from Batchelder's ninth grade went on to Reading High School, but only twenty-four of those graduated from high school. "Reading was tough," Barbara remembered. "We, from North Reading, stood out like sore thumbs, and they treated us terribly."

Nancy Ferretti recalled, however, that Barbara was voted prettiest girl in the class. "She looked just like Jean Tierney, the actress. I still think she is the prettiest! Did you know she went to a high school prom with Billy Smith (North Reading selectman)?"

Because her mother did not drive, Barbara often took the public bus that stopped at the corner of Park and Main. Public transportation allowed her to work at the Reading Diner, washing dishes from the time she was twelve. "I never could eat chicken croquettes or sausage after I saw what went into them," said Barbara.

"Coffee had just gone up to ten cents a cup. I worked at the Reading Diner until I graduated from high school; it got me out of that terrible shyness." During those years, her mother also waitressed at the Reading Diner and at the Red Hill Country Club, now the Hillview.

Barbara took the business course at Reading High School, hers the last class to graduate out of the building on Sanborn Street that is now condominiums. Mrs. Fransen, North Reading police officer Butchie Fransen's aunt, was a terrific shorthand teacher, but Elizabeth Batchelder's English class bored her to tears. "We read *Silas Marner* for three years; I hated that book."

Barbara regrets she never got to take Helen Zimmerman's biology course like her husband, Nick, did. "Zimmie's classes were so much fun, but because I was in the business course they would not allow it." Elizabeth Batchelder and Helen Zimmerman lived for years on Tower Hill Road in North Reading. "After Elizabeth died, Zimmie used to come to our house for Thanksgiving and Christmas dinner. Those two knew all the kids. Dickie Spindler (North Reading's retired DPW director) was one of Zimmie's favorite students—she talked about him all the time," said Barbara.

After jobs at the Reading Saving Bank, Boston Stove Foundry, and a secretarial position at Boston University's School of Public Relations and Communications, Barbara married Nick O'Brien in 1957. Nick's tour of duty as an Air Force pilot took the young couple to North Carolina and Texas, but after six months they returned to a little apartment on Washington Street. In 1960 they bought a cape at 55 Central Street. Then, in 1965, Nick and Barbara moved to 95 Park Street into a house and barn that Ebenezer Damon built. This home provided room not only for a growing family, but for a fire truck in the side yard, and a 1947 Commonwealth Skyranger airplane in the barn.

Ebenezer Damon owned the area of Sylvia Road and Williams Road in the early 1800s. With his brother, James, he built the Third Meeting House on the Common, and in 1917 he built the Damon Tavern for his brother David, who was its innkeeper and the town's first postmaster. The first North Reading Post Office was located in Damon Tavern, as was the town's first telephone switchboard.

In 1974 Barbara joined the Bicentennial Commission. "That's when I really got bit by this history bug," she said. Also a member of that committee, Sylvia Hurley had been an independent title examiner at the Registry of Deeds, and had a thorough understanding of the process by which one traces the history of antique homesteads. In conjunction with the bicentennial preparations, Madge Nickerson, Peggy Church, Barbara O'Brien and others organized and encouraged townspeople who were living in older homes to trace their houses' histories.

"It took me almost a year at the registry to find out that Damon built my house in 1845." She did not stop with her own house, however. Barbara documented many of the older homes on Elm Street, because of the careful documentation that Madge Nickerson did on her 1752 home at the corner of Turner Farms and Elm.

It was during Sylvia Hurley's research on Gordon and Pauline Hall's home on Upton Avenue, that Barbara realized the necessity of using primary source material. The inaccuracy of several secondary sources had complicated the research.

Francis Nurse and his sons had at one time owned three dwellings on Hall's property. Francis Nurse moved to North Reading from Salem after his mother, Rebecca "Goody" Nurse was hanged as a Salem witch in 1692. Sylvia Hurley discovered that Francis's property transactions were recorded in the registry long after the actual sales. Since the information was not in chronological sequence, the dating of those dwellings had been problematical.

A month ago Barbara made a ten-page outline of her history of North Reading on a legal pad. "My son is selling me his old computer, and I am turning his old bedroom into an office," she said. Barbara will start her history from 1644, "the beginning of the beginning" as she refers to it, when Lynn Village became the town of Reading.

In 1651 Reading annexed a two-mile grant north of the Ipswich River that extended to the Andover line. In 1853 this granted land, and the area south of the river known as Sudler's Neck, was to separate and become the town of North Reading.

Tom Parker, first chair of the Historical Commission, has served on many committees with Barbara. "Barbara really has devoted an extraordinary amount of time to the preservation of historic properties in this town," said Tom. In his view, Ethel Little, Leo Murphy and Ed Leary were compilers of information about North Reading, but the only person who actually attempted a history of the town up to now was the Reverend Samuel LePage, who completed his work in 1944.

"The earliest writings about North Reading have been a mere footnote; I think the book is terribly exciting," he said.

"I want to tell this story from North Reading's point of view," said Barbara. There will undoubtedly be a section on the history of old houses and their occupants, and information about the gristmills, the saw mills, the Abbott Shoe Factory, the early settlers. Barbara wants to learn more about the early mills owned by the Flints, and John Phelps' mill on the Middletown line. "There still is a lot of research for me to do," she said. Barbara would also like to make a version of her book appropriate to school-age children; her own children have agreed to illustrate it.

—March 1, 1999

Hillview Country Club

"This place is a gem, a real gem," commented George Stack "As we climb in to one of the sixty golf carts at the Hillview Country Club for a tour of all eighteen holes on a crisp September afternoon. George is a member of the Hillview Commission, a board appointed by the North Reading Selectmen to oversee the 140-acre municipal golf course and clubhouse on North Street.

Appointed in 1987 to the Hillview Study Committee, George Stack and Police Chief Henry Purnell are both still serving on the Hillview Commission after thirteen years. Every two weeks George Stack, Chief Purnell and five other members of the Hillview Commission meet to plan capital improvements, set policy, and make sure all is running smoothly. The other five commissioners are Bob Mauceri, Jack Collins, Larry Dyment, Doug Doskocil and Steve O'Leary. "In the last thirteen years, a half a million people have played golf here. There are about 42,000 rounds of golf played per year," said George Stack.

On November 5, 1941, the property on North Street first incorporated as The Olde Redding Country Club. According to Barbara O'Brien, Harvey Kelch owned and operated it. "Harvey took a fancy to me," said Barbara. "I played with his daughter Valerie. Valerie and I would often dive for golf balls; Harvey paid us a nickel a ball. We were instructed never to give the retrieved balls to the players."

Barbara's mother worked as a waitress at the Red Hill Country Club. "Everyone went there—I don't think you had to be a member." Barbara recalled a huge veranda and elaborate front and side doors to the building. "It was famous for its mile-high sandwiches. They were inches high, and you could get them right at the bar. I never could eat a whole one. Lucky if I could finish a quarter," she said.

If you look carefully at the building today you will notice it grew by extensions and additions. On the left as you face the building is the original house, built in the early 1800s by Benjamin Holt. This being his home, Benjamin Holt owned perhaps a thousand acres along what is now North Street. He is thought to have made his money farming hops and selling wild pigeons he caught. On the two chimneys of the house are the letters R and H in raised brick, for "Red Hill," and presumably added in the twentieth century.

While there are few wild pigeons today on the golf course, the wild geese have taken up residence. Protecting the natural ecology of the property is a high priority for the Hillview Commission. When white pine trees had to be removed from the contiguous Plouff Avenue subdivision, the Hillview replanted all the trees, many of them on the Central Street side of the course.

"We only lost one tree," remarked George Stack. "I don't play much golf, to be honest with you. My zealousness for this is in the facility," he said. Impatiens flower around many trees, and holes 6, 12 and 15 have been completely rebuilt to make them longer, more interesting to play and more attractive. There is a white fenced area beyond the driving range, a grass nursery for the greens. The management group contracted to run the golf course provides a level 1-A golf pro and a certified greenskeeper.

Three pros in all, Chris Carter, Dick Baker and Erik Sorensen provide coaching and golf classes; and they also run the pro shop. Having graduated in 1999 from Salem State, Erik had golf practices and tournaments on this course when he attended North Reading High School. As we continue our tour in the golf cart, we observe a high school match in progress. Both North Reading and Wilmington High School teams still use the Hillview as their home course at no cost.

How did the town come to own this 140 acres of prime recreational land? Although no records are on file showing the exact date of the transfer, sometime in the 1950s the Red Hill Country Club sold to the Hillview Country Club, for members only. In the Hillview Commission's boardroom is a photo taken during that decade with guest James Garner of Maverick fame drawing quite a crowd near the swimming pool.

By the 1980s the club was in disrepair and had fallen on hard times. Sometime after new owner and manager Arthur Angelopulos bought the facility in 1984, he began making plans with a Boston developer to convert the space to a nine-hole golf course. One set of plans included building 110 single family homes along Central Street; another plan would have put 350 units of low/moderate income housing on the north side of the course.

"I remember speaking with Selectman Gerry Brooks at the time," said George Stack. "He wondered if I would be willing to serve on a study commission. The makeup of that original group was really paramount to the success of the project. There was major talent at that table."

"We were unusual," recalls Attorney Walter Bilowz, one of the original seven members, "in the sense that we would not ask the town for money except a couple hundred thousand to start up. The rest of the cost came out of bonds paid off by fees generated by the golf and function hall profits. And we did it!" There were two attorneys, Walter and James Senior, in addition to businessman Francis Hachey, contractor Michael Walsh, Police Chief Henry Purnell, Boston school administrator George Stack, and engineer William O'Brien.

"Bill O'Brien was a financial genius," said Walter. "Without him the financial success would not have been possible—his work was masterful." But each brought very special gifts. "Hank was around, available, able to check to be sure the work was getting done," said Walter. "Mike Walsh did extensive initial repair in the function hall. It was in terrible shape. Sometimes he'd be there at three in the morning fixing electrical problems. Ernie Doucette appointed the perfect committee," said Walter.

It was a demanding eight months. The committee met in the old town hall on the third floor (now the Flint Library) four nights a week. "We worked our tails off," said Walter. On January 19, 1988, the committee presented their proposal to a special town meeting. With 651 registered voters present, the committee moved to authorize the selectmen "to acquire by purchase or take by eminent domain the land known as Hillview Country Club." The vote was close to unanimously in favor on all articles.

Stringent rules govern the taking of land by eminent domain. North Reading's stated purpose for the taking of the Hillview property was twofold: to protect the aquifer of the Central Street well on which the property sits, and to preserve open space, especially open space for recreational use.

With approval of the state legislature, the commission established an enterprise account. If the enterprise in this type of account generates funds in excess of its fees, the golfing fees must be reduced or the money put into capital improvements. The money can never be put directly into the general funds of the town without violating the stipulations of the agreement.

After that town meeting in January 1988, the commission applied for a 1.5 million dollar grant from the Commonwealth and borrowed 6.8 million in bonds to be paid off in fifteen years. The state awarded the project 1.6 million.

"There are strings attached to the 1.6 million grant, but they are not burdensome strings," said Stack. In fact, it is really in the best interest of the town not to pay back this grant because it guarantees the space remain open and the aquifer safe. The original $200,000 borrowed from the town was paid back in the first year. "We did not negatively impact the tax rate in the town by one dollar," commented Fran Hachey, an original commissioner.

In April 1988, the commission hired Urilla Cheverie to serve as its operations manager. Working a mere twenty-two hours per week, she is still the only town employee on the premises. "I am so proud of what we do. I get excited by the success of it. We get a lot of calls from other towns, and we've been able to help them get started." It is frustrating to her that some people still think the Hillview is private. " 'Can *anyone* eat in the Pub?' they want to know," she said.

Good economic times and the popularity of recreational golf have allowed for constant improvement of the facility and an increasing surplus. How to handle the surplus?

Five years ago, Walter Bilowz and Bill O'Brien drew up some plans for recreational use of the Drinkwater/Central Street property that was coming up for sale. "This was one idea. Someone might have a better one. I wanted the committee to look into it," said Walter Bilowz. "After an open meeting I was approached by soccer people who were excited by the Ipswich River Park plan."

Walter drafted a motion to form the land utilization committee (LUC), and Mark Harmeling, who subsequently became LUC chair, presented the motion at town meeting.

Soon the LUC, like the Hillview Committee before it, was meeting many times a week to give birth to another great recreational resource for North Reading. Funded by the surplus from the municipal golf course, and financially under the umbrella of Hillview Enterprise, the Ipswich River Park, with its paths and soccer fields, tennis courts and street hockey rink, jungle gyms and picnic areas, is available to all of us because of the hard work and dedication of many volunteers.

"Rita Mullin and Margi Salt worked endlessly on this project," said Walter. "Margi did all the grant applications; she applied for, and got, one million dollars from the Commonwealth." Walter Bilowz praises Rita Mullin for following through on the Commissioner's Cup Golf Tournament just played October 1 to benefit the IRP. This is the seventh year of that fund-raiser.

Although he is in the process of selling his home and retiring to Cape Cod, Walter is still thinking of ways to enhance the quality of life in North Reading. In 2005 the bonds from the original debt of 6.8 million will be paid off. The Hillview Enterprise will then most likely be generating money in excess of million per year. What are we going to do with it? Reduce golfing fees? Make more capital improvements to the properties? Expand the enterprise?

Because of the benefit to the town, Attorney Bilowz would recommend all existing recreational land and any potential recreational land become part of the Hillview Enterprise. "If the enterprise is expanded by taking properties into it, then money, in lieu of taxes, can be paid to the town," he said. A green belt of conservation land along the Ipswich River, a pool, a skating rink, a field house—anything would be possible. "If you have a better idea, I'd like to hear it," he said.

"All of us are glad we had the opportunity to do what we did," said Walter. "We did what was right for the town. Success is its own reward. I look with pride at the result. The Ipswich River Park is the crown jewel of Hillview."

—*October 6, 2000*

Martins Pond Turtle Walk

In 1900 streetcars made their debut in North Reading, allowing Bostonians easy access to the country. The bumpy ride to Martins Pond on the trolley tracks along Route 28 took two hours and cost ten cents for adults, five cents for children. The trolley stopped at Holt's Grove near Batchelder Avenue. This and other facts are now catalogued and explained on the new Turtle Trail that made its debut, July 25, at the fourth annual Martins Pond Summer Festival and Fishing Derby.

The Clarke Park Turtle Trail is a small water quality basin, and a 700-foot interpretive walk in the heart shape of Martins Pond. Stenciled turtles on the pathway tell the story of the Pond from otters to

Arrow Man to 1920s speakeasies, with vignettes of natural and human history referenced by numbers on the backs of painted turtles. The basin itself filters road and parking lot runoff before it enters the pond. In the winter the area will serve as a small skating rink before the pond freezes deeply enough to be safe. Visitors can also use the path for roller skating, stroller pushing and bicycling.

"Most environmental problems are caused by people; the solutions to these problems are, again, people and lifestyle," says Terry Bastian, whose business, Water Flowers, creates ecological design for golf courses, parks and private residences.

Terry, a member of the Martins Pond Association Playground Committee for six years, has donated his ecological and design expertise, and attends meetings to coordinate efforts with the Ipswich River Watershed Association's Stream Team Program. In addition to recreational and educational concerns, Terry's focus sometimes turns to issues of eutrophication (gradual filling in), phosphates and Title V septic specifications.

Martins Pond Association committee members work year-round on pond betterment. Meeting to plan a festival of burgers, watermelon, pony rides, live music, pie-eating contests, moon bounce, dog obedience demo and more, include: Terry Bastian, Lida Jenney, Janet Nicosia, Kathy Bakinowski, Harvey Card, Donna Colebrook, Julie and Dayle Colton, Bob and Donna Cyr, Joyce Davis, Rich Wallner, Margaret Geoffrion, Ray Holden, Kari Kilroy, Fran Mitchell, and Scott Ronco. Funds from these planned activities directly benefit park and pond improvement.

In 1997 the committee received confirmation that the Massachusetts Department of Environmental Management had selected the Turtle Trail project to receive a $4,000 matching grant, funded by the Massachusetts Lake and Pond Grant Program. Two thousand dollars of the matching money will come from North Reading's Martins Pond Study Committee account, and the another $2,000 will come from funds raised by the committee at their three annual events: the February Winter Festival, the July Summer Festival and the October Children's Haunted Playground. In December 1995 the North Reading Business Association donated $3,500 to park development, funds that have helped to develop the Turtle Trail.

"The festivals are so much fun for the whole family, and the projects have empowered us," says Lida Jenney, mother of two small children and co-chair of the committee with Janet Nicosia. "It is so rewarding to see the accomplishments of friends and to have the support of the North Reading business community." Boston Market has given cobblestones; Viking Tree regularly donates wood chips. Reading Municipal Light has installed new lighting fixtures to keep the park safe in the evening hours.

Volunteers have helped in so many ways. "The key is ownership," believes Terry. "People care about and for the Clarke Park because it is really theirs." Last April 26 (1997), volunteers raked, picked up trash, pruned, and painted. In June 1997 the committee hired a local contractor to make concrete repairs to the beach building in preparation for the painting of a new mural. On June 8, Jack and Joyce Vasapoli, with fourteen volunteers, began the painting of this new mural over the badly faded and peeling one they had designed and painted fifteen years ago.

Janet, a member of the committee since 1992, has helped to lobby for Clarke Park. She has spent endless hours along with Lida, Terry and others, researching the historic and ecological information needed for the Turtle Trail pamphlet.

Martins Pond was named in 1653 for William Martin, farmer, surveyor and town selectman. Acquiring his first fourteen acres from the Meadow Grant of 1647, his 188-acre farm near the pond covered much of the area by 1686 when smallpox reduced the Massachusetts tribe to less than 100. That year Native-American David Kunkshamooshaw sold the remaining Indian lands for fifty-five dollars.

Did you know that the Upton family built an icehouse at Holt's Grove to store and sell ice harvested from the pond?

Did you know the Skug River enters the pond from the north? That enough water flows through the pond to empty and fill it every eighteen days? That skug is the Native American name for skunk?

And why is the water so murky? At the deepest point the pond is only 7.25-feet deep with as much as ten feet of sediment below that. Sediment occupies seventy percent of the original basin, which was formed by the ice age 11,000 years ago.

Did you know that Malden-Essex Turnpike (now Route 28), built in 1806, was the main highway between Boston and New Hampshire until Route 93 was built in the 1950s? Paralleling Route 28 was the Salem and Lowell Railroad that sent the first locomotive, *Sailor Boy,* down its tracks in 1850, making the pond more accessible to city tourists.

This and more information on pond wildlife and pond history is available to all in the Turtle Trail guide near the message board at Clarke Park.

Three days after workers poured the Turtle Trail asphalt, Fran Mitchell visited Clarke Park in the early morning. To his great astonishment the trail was already in use. Before his very eyes a huge snapping turtle lumbered along the path toward the water. With the goal of "adapting people to nature instead of adapting nature to people," pond volunteers are glad to see that heron, kingbird, perch, muskrat, spotted salamander and even turtles still call Martins Pond home.

—July 24, 1998

Three

A Parade of Elections and Holidays

Damon Tavern, 1817, also known as the Weeks Building

Good Fences Make Good Neighbors?
Elect Don Roberts, Fence Viewer

It's the first week in November. Election signs for Cellucci and Harshbarger, Tierney and Torkildsen appear like fall pumpkins up and down Haverhill Street. In front of one house a sign reads: ELECT DON ROBERTS—FENCE VIEWER, TREE WARDEN.

Hasn't this very sign graced this lawn since the May elections seven months ago? Is the man still running? Don Roberts, five-year selectman in the early 1960s and two-year chair of that illustrious board, last May campaigned door-to-door on his bicycle for a position that no longer exists—fence viewer. It was his way of keeping before the public an issue that in his opinion has jeopardized his daughter Ruth's Route 28 business, The Vinery.

Born in Reading, Don Roberts moved to a small North Reading ranch house near the Thompson Country Club in 1951 with his bride, Sally. Just out of the Air Force, with a talent for repairing small appliances, Don opened a store a few doors from the current Hornet's Nest sub shop. Elmer Jones had a grocery store, and his brother Jack Jones had a hardware store in that same block; there was also a Rexall Drug.

"The Jones brothers were men of their word. The most honest and sincere persons I ever met. I went to school with Elmer's boy, Kenny," remembers Don. His first establishment, Strebor Stores (Roberts spelled backwards) sold clothing and shoes. After about a year Roberts moved to a location on Main Street near Tony Perry's trailer park.

"Through your life there is always someone who gives you a helping hand. Some months Perry would just say 'forget the rent.' He knew I was struggling." In those days Don typically opened at 8:00 A.M. and got home at eleven at night. "I worked seven days a week. I didn't know any better."

Don's father also owned a business on Route 28, the H. L. Roberts Company, located in what is now the Gonsalves building. Originally next to Harrows in Reading, the business moved to North Reading in 1954. H. L. Roberts was in business over fifty years. "My father sold nuts and bolts, fingernail polish, Kotex. A regular Spaggs. He put on quite a show."

Don Roberts' daughter Ruth, oldest of his five children, remembers working for her grandfather from the time she was eight. "I worked for a quarter," muses Ruth, a shop owner now herself. "My grandfather's store was a blast. He had a room full of monkeys. One was named Strebor. It was a typical country store. People would bring in their puppies and kittens. For two cents a pound they'd all have homes by the end of the day."

In 1955 Don put up the building next to his father's on land his father sold him, and began to market paint, toys, school supplies and, in 1970, swimming pool equipment. "When you don't know anything you keep plugging along." Don has fond memories of Mr. Gonsalves who bought the property from his father. According to Don, Gonsalves was truly a man of his word. "My father used to own twenty acres, all the way down to Nick O'Brien's gas station and back into the woods. When my father sold me the property he never gave me the deed. Part of my building was not on my land. Gonsalves knew this. I had to trust him. After he bought the land he walked right into my store with the deed, 'Just give me a dollar,' he said. He saved my life."

Seven years ago Don's daughter, Ruth Zarach, opened The Vinery. Her interior decorating, antique, and dried flower business occupies the same building Don built in 1955. "The bulk of my business is custom, personalized work. My father's store had a potbelly stove; friends always dropped by." Ruth also runs a friendly, service-oriented establishment. But her cozy, eucalyptus-scented store needs major renovation. "Come by on a rainy day; there are buckets everywhere," she laments.

Ruth spent $14,000 drawing up plans for a new building, and expected the old building would come down a year ago. A little over a year ago Ranger Development broke ground for fifty-six condominium units directly behind and to the south of The Vinery. Buyers must be fifty-five years of age or older, but this is an active adult community, not assisted living. At Northridge Estates, units with two bedrooms and two baths start at an affordable $179,000, according to Century 21 Realtor Joyce Spindler, who is already marketing the fifth phase. Last fall the developer planted tall pine trees along the access road that obscure Ruth Zarach's business.

"I'm for the project out back. It's a good use of the land," says Ruth. "I went to every meeting. My question was always 'What are your plans for the entrance?' They blew me off ... I wouldn't be opposed to smaller trees, but I've lost fifty percent of my business. Customers can't see me."

Realtor Joyce Spindler says, "The contractor did not plant the trees to hide the building; he did it to make an entry into Northridge. Mr. Roberts has tried every avenue to make the builder look bad."

The builder, Dave Murray of Ranger Development, did not return our calls. Bob Rogers, North Reading's town planner for the past nine years, explained that it is a civil matter between the two parties. "When the condo went in next door, the developer did not like the way Don's business looked; he put up trees as a barrier," recalls Bob. "The Board of Appeals did not require Northridge to show landscaping plans, and that's where the initial argument came from."

Peter Skerrett, member of the Board of Appeals confirmed that the subject of landscaping for the roadway into the development was not part of the hearing. "It was a wetlands review and, basically, we were interested in the engineering, the reports from Conservation, and from the Board of Health. He (Don) did not bring up the subject of landscaping—no one did." Don contends that the entry plans only showed grass.

The selectmen have appointed Peter to the board of appeals for the last thirty years. He has attended over 1,000 property-zoning meetings. Peter also served on the charter committee twenty-six years ago that eliminated the elected position of fence viewer. Wakefield and Newton are two towns that still have fence viewers, but there are not many left.

F. Leo DeLory has served as one of the three fence viewers for the town of Wakefield for the last ten years. Fence viewers go back to Colonial times, F. Leo DeLory said, to disputes about pastures in rural areas. "In Wakefield we resolve fifteen to twenty fence disputes per year. It's amazing sometimes—the lack of civility between neighbors."

Ironically, Sally Roberts, Don's wife, was one of North Reading's last fence viewers. She decided to be a write-in candidate in 1962 when the position was uncontested, and won handily with sixteen votes.

The following year, her name printed on the ballot as an incumbent, she received 1,800 votes. At the time fence viewers earned five dollars per viewing. "I wanted to make just five dollars so I could say I made more than Don did as selectman, which, of course, was nothing."

During two years in the position she only got one call. When the property owner found he had to pay five dollars, he canceled his request. She, like her selectman husband, never earned a penny in her elected position.

Don is still not sure how many votes he got for the nonexistent fence viewing position last May. How long will he keep his sign up? Maybe until lawyers resolve the dispute. Maybe until the trees are replaced with smaller ones. Maybe until next May's election.

"Most things that happen are for the best," says Don. "I can't remember any bad experience that didn't have some good come of it. But you stew about these things."

—November 6, 1998

Klaus Kubliersky, Town Moderator

The first time I brought the gavel down my heart was "right in my throat," remembers Klaus Kubliersky, town moderator for North Reading since 1984. "After five minutes, however, I was too busy conducting the meeting. You know, the secret to almost anything is to worry about what you are doing, and you'll stop worrying about yourself."

Klaus moved to North Reading in 1965, the very day his son, Ted, was born. His boss at Transitron, a semiconductor business in Wakefield, was selling a home in North Reading for a "reasonable" price. Klaus had completed his degree at Massachusetts Institute of

Technology the previous year and needed more space for his growing family than the Brookline apartment afforded.

Behind the Kubiersky home was some town-owned land that Klaus wanted to buy. Because such a purchase needed approval of the Board of Selectmen, Klaus sat through board deliberations one evening, waiting to voice his request. As he listened he realized, "These are the people who are making decisions about my town." He soon became a regular visitor, listening to the discussions of such leaders as Walter Bilowz, Charlie Statuti and Don Roberts, who where selectmen at the time.

"Someone noticed me there, showing an interest." Then, in early 1967, Jack Berenholtz, the chairman of the Board of Public Works, asked Klaus if he would serve on the refuse disposal committee. "Everyone with a sense of humor called it the 'garbage committee,' " recalls Klaus.

At that time the town had acquired 140 acres that included the current recycling center and dog pound. The plan was to move the dump from the Park Street location (near Chestnut Street—there is a playground there now) to this spot behind Moynihan Lumber. But there were environmental concerns because of the proximity of the Ipswich River. Klaus's service on the "garbage committee" led to appointment on the capital outlay committee, a group mandated to plan expenditure of capital funds to maintain a reasonable flow of debt for the town. This group projected population growth and advised on the spacing of town purchases.

Next he filled a vacancy on the Board of Public Works. When the town adopted its first charter in 1970, the public works department became appointed rather than elected. "That put me out of a job," remembers Klaus.

So he decided to run for town moderator. After filing his election papers, Klaus remembers thinking, "What have I done? I might get elected, and then I would have to be the moderator." Running against Peter Pijoan, Bob Schoolcraft and Paul Vergakes, Klaus launched a door-to-door campaign, explaining the role of town meeting and the job of moderator to the average citizen. And he won. "But not by much. I had 533 votes and Paul Vergakes got 471. It was a very close race."

Commuting to Cambridge at the time to work for American Science and Engineering, Klaus studied *Robert's Rules of Order* on the train. At the same time that he was reviewing that volume, a committee chaired by Al Sylvia Sr., was preparing chapter 11 of the town bylaws that govern the procedural conduct of town meeting. "My first job at town meeting was to supervise the adoption of these bylaws! In retrospect, Al Sylvia did a good job; the bylaws have served us well."

Taking a new direction in the fall of 1972, Klaus ran for North Reading selectman, a position he held until 1978. "No matter how much work I did on that board, I always felt guilty about not doing more." In 1980 and 1982 Klaus again ran for town moderator. This time, however, he lost to Steve O'Leary.

"You have no business running for public office if you are not able to accept defeat graciously," he believes. "The first five minutes after you lose are rough. But then sometimes you say, 'Thank God, I lost; it's someone else's problem.'" He has also made two unsuccessful races recently for the State Senate—both when he realized there was no contender on the Democratic slate against Republican Bruce Tarr. The first was a write-in campaign, which he won, subsequently losing in the general election with 20,000 votes. "I fared better than I expected," recalls Klaus. In 1984 he decided to throw his hat in the ring for moderator again; North Reading has been electing him to that position ever since.

"The primary reason I do it is so I can stay involved in town affairs. Serving as moderator is motivation to be aware of what is going on in town." There is a private sector and a public sector to our country. Klaus believes that there must be a balance between the two.

"We cannot live without that public sector," he says.

He came to this country with his half-sister, Juliana; half-brother Michael and his mother in 1951. His stepfather, after serving as a Hungarian diplomat in Italy during World War II and then, as press attaché to the Vatican, had moved to New York City in 1948 because of his job with Voice of America and Radio Free Europe.

As a German child living in Milan at the time of the first air raid, and also present in Rome in 1944 when the Americans arrived at the end of the war, Klaus has given considerable thought to why people go to war. He has often wondered what the world might be like without war. Does war perform a useful function, perhaps, breaking patterns that have become so constrictive there is no room for progress?

In retrospect the events of the war were more traumatic to him than they were at the time. Perhaps the strong influence of his mother contributed to his sense of well being during those years.

"My mother was very much interested in the world," he says. Deeply committed to sculpture, she had her own exhibit in Rome in the early 1950s after the family moved to New York City. His mother had nearly completed her premed studies prior to meeting Klaus's father, who died in Argentina when Klaus was only three years old. Klaus remembers an Italian saying: A person is worth as much as he knows. The Kubiersky family has always deeply valued education and knowledge.

Having served for so many years in town government, does he ever tire of the town moderator position? "It is never dull. There are always new faces, new issues. As my eyesight gets worse, it is a challenge to see the faces at the rear of the auditorium. I have been known to call on the gentleman in the back row, and then discover he is a lady. And, worse yet, my neighbor!"

—October 2, 1998

Betty Vullo, Justice of the Peace and Town Clerk for Thirty Years

There is a certain charm to that Norman Rockwell *Saturday Evening Post* cover of the young couple standing before the justice of the peace behind his high oak desk in a musty town hall of the 1950s. While blond and petite Betty Vullo does not quite fit the Rockwell image, she held the position of North Reading town clerk for almost thirty years, and received her justice of the peace commission in 1969.

Betty and John Vullo and their three young children moved to North Reading from Wichita, Kansas, when, in 1961, John took a job with Avco in Wilmington.

"When the twins entered junior high and Valerie was in high school, a friend told me the town clerk, Ruth Balick, was looking for part-time help. I applied and got the job." Soon after that Ruth had to resign because of poor health. In September 1969, the North Reading Selectmen appointed Betty to fill Ruth's unexpired term.

In the March 1970 election, Betty's name appeared on the ballot for the first and only time. The new town charter was also on that March 1970 ballot. The Home Rule Charter having passed, the position of town clerk became an appointed one rather than elected.

"I won the election," said Betty, "and I was immediately appointed by the town administrator as the new bylaws dictated."

There are over 300 chapters and sections of the Massachusetts General laws that detail the tasks of the town clerk. The clerk's primary duty is the facilitating and holding of elections. As chief election official for the town, Betty issued nomination papers, prepared the ballot, handled voter registration, the hiring of election workers, and the counting of ballots.

Voter registration requirements have changed dramatically since 1969 when new voters had to climb two flights of marble stairs in the Flint Building. Flint Memorial Hall currently houses the town library, but until 1990 it held the administrative offices for the town.

Betty's office was tucked into a corner behind four-drawer file cabinets, not bearing much resemblance to the Norman Rockwell graphic. To register to vote one had to have lived in North Reading for one year, be twenty-one years of age, show proper identification, and to be able to read a paragraph of the Constitution that Betty presented.

"When the age requirement changed to eighteen, I remember the first young man who came in to register was Ron Meshna. He had just had his birthday." The changes in voter registration in thirty years are drastic, according to Betty. Currently there is no residency-length requirement, no reading requirement; it is possible to register by mail. "But the system still survives and works pretty well," she said.

For the first twenty years that she was town clerk, North Reading did not own voting machines. In 1969 there was only one precinct, and all voting occurred in the Third Meeting House (the Building on the Common).

Since federal law mandates no more than 4,000 voters in a precinct, by the mid-1980s precincts had grown to four, with residents casting their votes in the high school gymnasium and at St. Theresa's parish hall. Betty was having increasing difficulty recruiting a team to count the paper ballots. After polls closed at 8:00 P.M., the counting process typically continued until five in the morning.

"I went to the town meeting twice and asked for voting machines. Twice the proposal was voted down." What to do? Betty decided to ask those who spoke most vehemently at town meeting against the machines to serve on the counting committee. "And that did it," she said. "We got our machines in 1988."

In addition to her duties as chief election official, the town clerk is responsible for recording all town meeting votes and sending them to the attorney general's office. She also posts announcements for meetings, elections and town office vacancies.

A third task of the town clerk is to issue vital records for the residents of the town: birth, marriage and death certificates. On any given day the town clerk's office may be asked to produce one of these documents dating from 1853, the year North Reading was incorporated, to the present. Records prior to 1853 are stored in Reading. The importance of the office in this area of vital records is diminishing as computers allow the state to centralize the process. As of January 1, 2000, vital records are issued directly from the state of Massachusetts.

The process for getting a marriage license remains the same as when Betty assumed her job. Bride and groom must get blood tests that are valid for thirty days. Valid for sixty days, a marriage certificate must be obtained at least three days prior to the wedding.

By virtue of being the town clerk, Betty applied in 1969 to be a justice of the peace. Some incorrectly assume a justice of the peace is a judge. While a judge might be a justice of the peace, a justice of the peace is not necessarily a judge. In some states the justice of the peace can hold court, levy fines and issue speeding tickets; but in Massachusetts, the justice of the peace's duties are to administer oaths of office, to take depositions or legal statements, to call town meetings, and to perform marriages.

To become a justice of the peace, one must get an application from the secretary of state, collect signatures attesting to one's good character from a judge, an attorney, two elected officials in the town, and two others. While there is no academic requirement, Betty graduated from the International Institute of Municipal Clerks, a program offered at Salve Regina College in Newport, Rhode Island. "The training was fascinating," she said. "It covered such areas as public speaking, how to deal with the public, whether it is better for clerks to be appointed or elected."

After the governor's council reviews and accepts the application and fee, the governor signs the document and the candidate goes to the Massachusetts State House to be sworn in. Governor Frank Sargent was in office when Betty received her first commission. Every seven years the justice of the peace must renew his or her license. Justice of the peace commissions are limited by the town's population; there may only be one JP per 5,000 residents.

In 1969, a justice of the peace could only perform weddings in her own town. For the first ten years, ninety percent of the couples Betty married, used her living room as their chapel.

One time, dressed in black leather, two couples rode up on their Harleys, the bride on the best man's machine, the groom and the maid-of-honor on the other motorcycle. After the ceremony, the bride and groom rode off together. "These were not kids; they were in their forties," said Betty.

The motorcycle couple had an appointment, but on another occasion Betty's doorbell rang, and standing before her were two young people who looked to be about sixteen years old. They had seen the justice of the peace sign on her house, and wanted to know if they could get married.

"Do you have your license?" Betty asked. The young man pulled out his driver's license. "No, I mean the marriage license," she said. They were so embarrassed. The bride-to-be said, "I told you, dummy." And they left.

One night the Vullos got a call at 9:00 P.M. from a couple whose sixty-day license was going to expire at midnight. "Can you marry us tonight?" they wanted to know. Betty agreed and gave them directions to her house.

Ten o'clock went by, then ten-thirty. Eleven o'clock came and went. At eleven-thirty, the phone rang. It was North Reading Police Sergeant Ed Denicourt.

"Betty, there is a couple here on Route 28 who are totally lost and trying to find your house. Are you expecting them?" he asked. Sergeant Denicourt not only escorted the young couple to Sunset Avenue, but also came in to serve as one of the two witnesses. "Wearing his plaid bathrobe, my husband John was the other witness. I was in my aqua-blue bathrobe. We finished the ceremony before midnight," said Betty.

After the law changed to allow JPs to perform marriages anywhere in the state, only about fifty percent of the weddings happened in the Vullo living room. Betty has tied the knot for couples on a cruise ship in Boston Harbor, at the New England Aquarium, in Copley Plaza and at the Hillview Country Club. She was also the officiant at the marriage of Bruin's hockey great, Tony Esposito, at his friend's home in North Reading.

On February 6, 1978, Betty traveled to Logan Airport to conduct services for an airplane pilot and his bride in the cockpit of the groom's plane. To her surprise, the family had notified the press about the event. When she arrived at Logan, news reporters with television cameras were milling about the terminal. The cockpit ceremony appeared on the ten o'clock news along side updates to the '78 blizzard conditions.

There are numerous reasons couples choose a JP over a church wedding, but Betty, having performed over one thousand weddings in the last thirty years, believes the primary ones are: marriages between faiths, weddings of divorced Catholics, and couples seeking a more modest cost.

"Using a justice of the peace is a way to keep it simple," she said.

Although she retired from her position of North Reading's town clerk in 1998, Betty is far from retired when it comes to weddings. "September is typically my busiest month. Sometimes there are three weddings in a weekend. It is such an upbeat and happy occasion. So nice to be a part of it."

—October 15, 1999

Martins Pond Haunted Playground

Bob Cyr called me during the week with 'I'm afraid it's not scary enough,' " reports Janet Nicosia referring to the Children's Haunted Playground, which opens at Martins Pond tomorrow night at 6:30 P.M. Especially planned for children from three to ten, young people up to age ninety will want to pay one dollar for their bat ring, and to tour Martins Grave, The Hall of Regret and Cannibal Cave. At 8:00 P.M., Frankenstein (North Reading High School student Ben Poirier) and his bride (Joyce Davis) invite one and all to their wedding procession through the Graveyard. Dress in costume; there will be prizes!

In its fourth year to benefit Clarke Park, this year's Haunted Playground expects to attract even more than the 400-500 visitors who came last year.

"It's a blast," says Janet. "Last year my husband and I were Frankenstein and the doctor, but this year we will be cannibals. We all get in the spirit of it." At least forty volunteers run the event on Saturday.

"Bob and Donna Cyr are a major driving force behind the scenes," says Janet. Bob will spend all day Saturday digging graves. This year the Cyrs are focusing special attention on the witches' brew caldron, which will have a smoke machine and green lights to give it that ghoulish look.

Josh Greenstein, a North Reading High School junior known for his talent as a magician, is directing the special effects in The Hall of Regret, where Greg Calafatos will play the devil. Purchase a lightrope necklace and follow a volunteer tour guide through The Hall of Regret, along the Turtle Trail to see the fortune teller and the newly donated guillotine, a visual effect staged by Jim and Debbie Luskotoff of Andover's Camp Evergreen.

Donna Colebrook will be coordinating the sale of hot chocolate and hot dogs, which Bob Berg has again generously provided. Moynihan Lumber has loaned its popcorn machine, and Sandy Wenzell will again dip all those red candy apples.

"Volunteers see something good and want to be part of it," says Janet. "We've been asked what you have to do to join. The answer is 'just show up.' "

—*October 23, 1998*

Apple Festival Encore

Saturday, September 26, 1998, the North Reading Historical and Antiquarian Society presents its fourth annual Apple Festival Encore on the lawn behind the Putnam House herb garden on Bow Street.

Some will attend primarily for their slice of homemade apple pie with a dollop of Richardson's homemade ice cream. The pies are served immediately following the blue ribbon results of the apple pie contest. Unbiased judges, usually town dignitaries, will award three ribbons at noon. The baking contest is open to all. Should you be reaching for the rolling pin, pies must be of the traditional sort: no raisins or cranberries or exotic spices.

There is a special category for children who bake. Bring competing pies to the Putnam House before 11:00 A.M.

Others will attend the event primarily for the art raffle. Over twenty local area artists have contributed their work, which has been on display at the North Reading Public Library for the month of September. On Saturday morning the artwork will move to the 1844 West Village School House behind the Putnam House. Raffle tickets may still be purchased for one dollar each, or six for five dollars. Drawing of the winners will occur at 2:00 P.M."

Since the Historical and Antiquarian Society's inception in 1953, the purpose of the group has been the "promotion of interest in articles of antiquity, their preservation and history."

The Historical Society has undertaken the restoration and supervision of several historic structures at no cost to the taxpayers. With a membership of close to 100, current dues for a family are twenty dollars; ten dollars for a senior citizen. The fall Apple Festival is the organization's primary fund-raiser.

A pressing need this year is a new roof for the 1910 barn, which stores, among other items, the Gowing family baby carriage, a sleigh, old farm implements and the sales model of an ice wagon built by MacLane, a North Reading carriage maker.

In 1720, the people of North Reading built the Reverend Daniel Putnam House for the first pastor of the parish. It was in 1717 that townspeople voted "to settle a minister amongst them as fast as they could and to ... give him ... twelve acres of land and 4 score pounds in building and manuring."

Reverend Daniel Putnam, a twenty-three-year-old graduate of Harvard's class of 1713, negotiated "20 acres of land ... an annual salary to be 15 cords of wood and 66 pounds of hard money." His house was to be "15 feet long, 19 feet wide and 15 feet stud, a lenter on the back side ... three chimneys from the ground ... a convenient parlor."

Originally the 1720 house had only the two rooms (up and down) to the right of the front door where the Reverend Putnam lived, serving as the town's pastor until his death on June 10, 1759. In 1795, the Putnam family added the two rooms to the left of the current front door. In 1820, the cooking lean-to in back was taken away and the current kitchen and front stairway added. Indoor plumbing and electricity were unobtrusively installed during the twentieth century.

Barbara Zarick, is one of the docents who were trained in the late 1950s by Bob Parker and Pat Romeo, points out, "You might think those early people were not so sharp. Reverend Putnam was no country bumpkin, however. He negotiated a house and grazing land, stipulating the house would be property of his family even when his ministry ended."

The Reverend Putnam's family remained in the house until the early 1950s when the last "Put" died. There was concern that the building would be razed, a convenience store replacing it. The desire to preserve it led to the founding of the Historical and Antiquarian Society by members of the Upland Club. These dedicated volunteers, including Peggy Parker, Barbara Zarick, Mary Walsh, Priscilla Ham, Barbara Munroe, Vivian Eisenhaure and Mildred Turner, transformed the Putnam House from an abandoned, partially burned structure inhabited by several raccoon families, into a carefully restored, early eighteenth-century family dwelling.

Over the past forty years, volunteers have sold afghans, made quilts to raffle, held old-fashioned strawberry festivals, sold pewter jewelry, T-shirts and mugs to fund repair of the buildings.

Mary Walsh has once again organized the raffle. Priscilla Drinkwater and Marian Thompson will handle the flea market, while Cheryl Wichmann and Cathy McDonnell oversee the craft tables. Twenty-five dollars buys you a table to sell your wares. Barbara Zarick has arranged for the "sitters" and docents to give tours and welcome guests into the Putnam House during the Apple Festival.

When Barbara and her husband first moved to North Reading in 1948 they co-owned the trailer park on Van Heusen Farm with Sam Bellino. Later the drive-in theater showed movies on that land; now Stop and Shop sells groceries there. There was a big house on that property next to Cronin's Garage, that at one time had been a stagecoach stop. Without understanding its worth, the owners had the house and its priceless Rufus Porter murals, similar to those in Damon Tavern, bulldozed and carted away.

"Later, I was sick about it," admits Barbara. She and others in the Historical and Antiquarian Society have been working hard ever since to preserve those treasures that are still ours to enjoy.

Ginny Mills chairs this year's Apple Festival as she has the last two. "It is a big committee and everyone does a lot of work all summer long," says Ginny. "I will wear my stupid apple core outfit again, with a leaf on my head. Everyone has a good time. It will happen rain or shine."

—September 25, 1998

Phil Norris and the North Reading Community Band

Peggy Church was taking bassoon lessons again in 1979 when Phil and Diane Norris moved across town to 240 Elm Street. One evening, sitting in Peggy's living room next door, the Norrises and the Churches got talking about the tenor saxophone in Phil's study closet, unplayed for fifteen years. Phil played piano for his own amusement, an occasional Gershwin tune or Dixieland standard, but the sax had not been out of the case since college. "What if we started a North Reading Community Band?" they plotted.

Peggy and Phil made a few phone calls, borrowed some intermediate selections: *Sound of Music,* "Zampa," and a march, "Americans We," from the high school collection, and then got permission from Agatha Marano, the North Reading Middle School music teacher, and Hal Weiss, the director of music in the North Reading Public Schools, to hold the first meeting in the high school band room.

A few years later Hal Weiss actually joined the group playing bass, not his primary instrument. Agatha came to the first rehearsal with her French horn, also not her primary instrument. Other early members included Barbara White, Chris Petty and the Cushing kids. "Tricia Cushing was a music major on baritone horn and trombone, but preferred to play clarinet with us," remembers Phil.

Debi Ham, clarinet, George Chabot, trumpet, Paul Lewis, primarily a sax player who plays tuba for the band, and Debi's sister, Betsy Ham Driscoll, flute, were all members of the original band who continue to play every Thursday night at 7:30 in the Middle School Large Group Room, almost twenty years later.

The North Reading Community Band gave its first performance in 1981 when the tradition of Christmas on the Common was in its infancy, as was the ten to fifteen-piece band.

"The forces of darkness and disorder always seemed to be conspiring to deep-six that Christmas concert," recalls Phil. One year a member had a minor car accident en route; another time the bass player had tickets to *Cats*. But the worst had to be the year Cheryl Billings, the conductor and Peggy's bassoon teacher, was eight months pregnant with Rh factor complications.

"When I got a call on Friday night that Cheryl had been hauled into the hospital, we not only needed a replacement conductor, some of our parts for "Silent Night" and "White Christmas" were in a canvas bag in Cheryl's front hall in Danvers. Agatha retrieved the conductor's scores on her way up from Lynn, so that she could study them sufficiently to share the baton with Judith Allen, who taught flute lessons at the middle school and played in the infant band. Judith has been conducting the group ever since.

In the early years, Christian Community Service coordinated Christmas on the Common at the North Reading bandstand. Mary and Joseph arrived on a live donkey no matter how inclement the weather. After the crèche scene at the bandstand, the North Reading Community Band, along with the North Reading Community Chorale, entertained in Union Congregation Church parish hall, while the faithful warmed up with hot cocoa.

"We always managed to pull it off," remembers Phil. "Now it is almost on cruise control, but in the early days it was a hypertensive effort." In addition to its yearly appearance at Christmas on the Common, the North Reading Community Band plays at senior citizen homes, locally and in neighboring communities.

Middleton has invited the band to provide music on a number of occasions. "One year they wanted us to march in their parade. But we don't march. So they set us up in front of the library where the parade began. The parade went down Route 62 and back, and we just kept playing Sousa."

Like so many others in the band, Phil began to play his instrument in his teens. Unlike others who had the benefit of school music lessons, Phil was self-taught. DeLaSalle High School in Minneapolis had no music program. Phil's buddy, Bob Snow, had a dad who played in the Dorsey Band. By the time they were juniors, Bob and Phil had a combo together. They played Dixieland at New Year's Eve parties and school dances. Solo trumpeter in the American Legion Band, Bob roped Phil into playing sax there as well.

"That's where I really learned to read music. It's not rocket science to learn what a quarter note is worth, but it's something else to do it with the baton moving; I learned from other musicians. We traveled all over the state and as far away as Fargo, North Dakota, to march in parades."

As an undergraduate, Phil joined MIT's big band jazz group, the "Techtonians." He also had a combo, playing piano (self-taught) and sax. The combo played mostly at fraternity parties. Then Phil graduated, and the sax went into its case. Fifteen years later, his tenor sax had leaky pads and needed repair. When the North Reading band began, he borrowed an alto sax from Peggy Church's daughter, Laura, who played in Hal Weiss's high school marching band. "Much later I bought a nice Selmar Mark 6 from the *Want Advertiser*. Emilio at Rayburn's did the rehab."

The North Reading Community Band does not hold auditions. For the most part the process is self-selective. If musicians show up for rehearsals and find the music too difficult or not challenging enough they drop out. "If we don't plan enough events, attendance tends to wane," says Phil.

At one rehearsal many years ago at Town Hall, Terry Muskavitch and Phil were the only players who showed up. One flute and one saxophone is an interesting combination. "We actually held the rehearsal; we sang some of the cued parts."

Phil, by his own admission is "chief cook and bottle washer" for the North Reading Community Band. Co-founder, president, librarian, there is always a new challenge for him. "I had my conducting debut at the August 6 concert with Sousa's "Stars and Stripes," so that Judy could play the piccolo part. I've led bands, but I never used the stick before."

—July 21, 1998

Minitmen Again Lead the Memorial Day Parade

"To start at 10:00 A.M. exactly, and to keep everyone waiting in line—that is the challenge," Roy Walters mused last week, responsible, along with the North Reading Company of Minitmen and Militia, these twenty years for the Memorial Day Parade. And there he stood Monday, clipboard in hand, authentic pre-Revolutionary War attire, helping to put in order selectmen, parade Marshall (Dr. Bill Butler), veterans, Cub Scouts, high school band, Bookworms, Little Leaguers, decorated bicycles, antique cars, fire engines and ten floats.

Sadly, one of the floats was draped in black bunting, an emotional tribute to two of the Militia's loyal members who died this spring: Alan Holmes and James Stewart. The float carried Alan's musket and Jim's tricorne and drum, items they had carried themselves last Memorial Day. Because Jim had been elected captain just weeks before his death, the Minitmen marched with the captain spot empty.

"The company is reeling this spring from the double loss," lamented Geoff Bemis who walked into his first meeting in 1975, the same night Burt Kenty joined. For him it was a chance to be involved in remembering history. "It was a family thing, too," said Geoff, "My wife, Patty, made authentic attire for all of us." Six and ten years old in the Bicentennial year, Missy and Geoff Jr., also marched in many parades along with children in the Stewart and Walter families.

When the tall ships came for the first times in 1976, the Minitmen served as honor guard in Boston City Hall Plaza. "We had been instructed to stand at attention," Geoff remembered, "but as the mayor of Boston, Prince Phillip and Queen Elizabeth passed by, the queen stopped and spoke to Marilyn Holmes who, astonished, curtsied.

In those early years the Minitmen gave demonstrations in schools and at businesses. John Hancock even featured their picture on its 1976 calendar. Leaving another Boston event, a demo for the Kirby Vacuum Cleaner convention at the HoJo's in the theater district, the Militia, in Minitmen attire, marched back to the Hancock garage with muskets, drummers keeping the beat. Then Police Chief Gordon Berridge was a bit nervous marching by the Boston Police Station lacking permits for those pre-Revolutionary guns. But when they stopped at Whimsey's for dinner, the management wanted them to parade around the restaurant to entertain the customers.

In the 1970s there were many parades and reenactments. On April 18th, 1975, right here in North Reading, local citizens recreated the march to Concord. A local policeman, Ed Denicourt, dressed as Dr. John Brooks, rode through the crowd calling the militia to assemble. Following a display of manual arms, the Minitmen and ladies participated in a seventeenth century church service at the Union Congregational Church at which Reverend Harold Fohlin christened Cynthia Jean Miller in her grandfather's eyelet gown.

By 1977 some of the membership were losing interest in the re-enactments and parades—in fact many had dropped out after the Bicentennial celebration. Remaining members took responsibility for organizing the Memorial Day parade and held auctions to raise money for the Citizen's Scholarship Fund. In 1980 the group had a new challenge when the town bought McMillan's Garage, located at the corner of Main Street and Park, for one dollar. Because of its historical significance, Meltzer's furniture offered the building to the town rather than see it fall to the wrecking ball. After the original (called the Puddin' Point School) burned in 1840, the West Side Village School was rebuilt in 1845 where children gathered in this one room to learn to read and write until the early 1900s. In 1916 it became the Westside Village Branch of the Flint Memorial Library and subsequently McMillans' Garage. In agreeing to move and restore the schoolhouse, the Minitmen had a major project—a project that lasted fourteen years and three months.

First they gutted it, disassembled it, and chain-sawed it into pieces under the watchful and meticulous eye of historian and engineer Bob Parker. "Mr. Parker was very particular about how things needed to be," recalled charter member Gordon Hall. "We could only use authentic methods and materials." Potbelly stove, chalkboard, desks from the mid-1800s, even the school bell for the tower that George LaPerche found near York, Maine, added to its authenticity. In 1994 at the dedication, after a speech by Superintendent David Troughton, the school bell rang, calling the children to class, and Norma Stiles, middle school science teacher, reenacted an 1887 class in session.

The Minitmen continued to meet, hold a yearly auction, pancake breakfasts, Country and Western Dances raising money to maintain the building, and provide scholarships for local youth with a penchant for history. "But as time went on, we had to get back to our private lives—paint the house, clean the garage," remarked Minitman Walters. "The deaths this spring of Alan and Jim seem to have rekindled interest in earlier goals of the organization."

"Jim's dream was to have a mini-Sturbridge," added Geoff. "But his more immediate goal was to finish the restoration of the outbuilding, which had at one time been the privy."

—May 26, 1998

Warren Pearce Jr., Fourth of July's Pyrotecnician

It really scares me to death that he messes with it," says Holly, wife of Warren Pearce who, with three licensed pyrotechnicians, will set off North Reading's fireworks this Sunday, July 5. Because of Warren and a dedicated Fourth of July Committee, North Reading will have not only a bonfire, but also an impressive fireworks display for the fourth year in a row.

When Warren was a small boy growing up in North Reading, he remembers the magic of bonfires he attended with his eight siblings. Over the years Warren noticed that North Reading became a place you left to spend summer holidays in New Hampshire or on the Cape. Warren wanted his own four children and numerous foster children to experience the joy of an old-fashioned Fourth of July right here in town.

In 1976 the mammoth bonfire, made with wood donated by Viking Tree, drew an enthusiastic crowd. But the town-appointed Bicentennial Committee for the Fourth eventually disbanded. Four years ago with leadership from citizens such as Tanya Wulleman, Joanna Purnell, Rita Mullin and Warren Pearce, the dream of a hometown celebration with fireworks became a reality.

Warren gives credit to Joanna Purnell, a tireless worker. "I'd be lost with out her. She makes so many phone calls." The Fourth of July committee works all year to raise over $12,000, sponsoring a raffle and a Las Vegas Night. They successfully solicit donations from generous local merchants as well. Because the celebration is not a line item in the town budget, earning these funds becomes a year-long commitment for the committee.

In addition to the fireworks and bonfire, the committee has planned a 5-K road race, a dunk tank, an adult volleyball tournament, races for young children, carnival rides, karaoke, a karate demonstration, a play titled *Freedom,* and the announcement of North Reading's Citizen of the Year.

"There is so much to do and people are great, but it would be a lot more fun for me if there was more technical help with the fireworks," says Warren, who is also chairman of the Community Planning Commission, liaison to the J. T. Berry Re-use Committee, member of the Route 28 Study Committee and member of the original KIDSPOT construction team. Most recently he has been working to get House Bill 4052, the Concord Street Sewer District bill, filed. Warren is no stranger to civic responsibility.

The responsibility for bonfire and fireworks safety has led Warren to hours and weekends and years of training to become a licensed pyrotechnician. First he apprenticed to another technician from New Hampshire, attending numerous events to learn the skills. As a member of the New Hampshire Pyrotechnic Association (NHPA) he has training, competitions and conventions available to him year-round. The Commonwealth of Massachusetts requires tests on both the chemistry and safe handling of fireworks to be granted a license. Each state has separate licensing requirements for pyrotechnicians, and Massachusetts is one of the most stringent. North Reading always has had three pyrotechnicians on the scene for the fireworks and also for the cleanup. Holly explains that, on the day following the fireworks, the whole family picks up the shells on the football field. There are always a few rockets that did not ignite. "We never touch a live one. We mark them and call on the pyrotechnic guys," says Warren. "We try to make it better every year," says Warren. "The first question we always ask is, 'How can we make it safer next July?' The second question is, 'How can we make it more fun for everyone?'"

On the weekend of the Fourth, Warren will travel to Rockingham, New Hampshire, to buy the supplies to make fireworks and to purchase the already constructed Chinese pieces he needs. The construction of each individual rocket involves three elements: the kind of gunpowder (green dot, blue dot or red dot), the kind of metal (for example aluminum or magnesium), and the way these explosive materials are wrapped in cardboard and brown paper shell. Some are the size of candlepin bowling balls, while others are six or twelve-inch rods.

Which are Warren's favorites? "I like the ones with the little magnesium stars on the string. They twinkle when they light up the sky." Various pyrotechnic associations hold competitions for unique fireworks creations. Imagine if your artist's palette were the sky. Is Warren thinking of entering such contests? "No," he says, "I'm still a novice; I'm still learning."

—July 3, 1998

Mary Rubenstein's Fascination with Clara Louise Burnham

For almost thirty years Mary Rubenstein has been collecting the novels and short stories of Clara Louise Burnham.

"Last week for the first time in my entire life I was in a room with other people who had read her books!" exclaimed Mary after the North Reading Book Discussion Group met in the Flint Library Activity Room with fourteen attending.

Mary's interest in romance novelist Burnham (1854–1927) began in 1970. The United States Navy had just transferred her husband, Ralph, to Boston from Monterey, and the Rubensteins had bought a house on Woodland Drive.

Interested in local history, Mary had read about this local author in the Reverend LePage's *History of North Reading*. One day, as Mary looked over a table of used books near the fireplace in the old library building (Damon Tavern), she spotted a book by Burnham for ten cents. Excited by her find, she took the book, *In Apple Blossom Time*, to the circulation desk.

"Clara Louise Burnham was George Root's daughter, you know," volunteered library worker Ruth Beacom. And so Mary's collection, now numbering thirty volumes, began.

Burnham's father, George Root (1820–1895) was a composer, music publisher and teacher. Buried at Harmony Vale Cemetery where Burnham also has her stone, Root is best remembered for his Civil War songs, "Tramp, Tramp, Tramp, the Boys Are Marching," "Just Before the Battle, Mother" and "Battle Cry of Freedom."

Born in Sheffield, Massachusetts, George Root, at the age of six, moved to Willow Farm on Haverhill Street, which in the 1890s became Eisenhaure Farm. Root's parents, Sarah Flint and Frederick Root, lived and farmed this property until 1870 when Frederick passed away.

George Root's autobiography, *A Musical Life,* available in the North Reading Library history room and in the biography section, tells of Root's return from New York City to North Reading in the 1850s to found a summer school for choral music teachers.

North Reading "called a town meeting at which was explained that the school would probably bring a hundred strangers there for three months which would mean to the town some money and a good deal of music. Both ideas were well-received and prompt action was taken," writes George Root in his book. The town made some renovations to the Third Meeting House; the Uptons loaned their pump organ; other families near the center of town set up their homes to take in boarders. The school ran four summers bringing music and revenue to the town.

When Clara Louise was nine years old, her father moved his family to Chicago to join a music publishing business with his brother: Root & Cady. The ties to North Reading, however, remained strong. Clara had been baptized at the Union Congregational Church, which both her Flint and Root grandfathers had had a hand at building. Because her grandparents still lived at Willow Farm, Clara returned to summer here. The rural farm life of North Reading figures prominently in her nostalgic novels that were first published in 1881 by Sumner & Co., a publishing house across the street from her father's business in Chicago. Soon Houghton Mifflin picked up her stories; she was a best seller for them. A 1910 catalogue for Houghton Mifflin features her new book *Clever Betsy* on its cover. Selling for $1.25 with twelve cents postage:

"This happy love story tells how Clever Betsy, a shrewd, yet likable spinster, did a good turn for Rosalie Vincent. It takes the reader to the wonderful Yellowstone National Park as well as to the Maine coast," advertises the early brochure. Clara Louise Burnham pictures a staid and moral society without the excesses of modern times," observes LePage in his 1944 North Reading history.

Clara's characters sometimes mirror her own family members and issues. Perhaps because she was a high-class Flint, Clara creates a proud character who says, "You can compare grandmothers with the best of them."

Another character, a singer, gives up marriage to pursue a singing career; one of Clara's aunts, similarly, gave up a musical career because of her husband's opposition.

A rural train station is an important part of the setting in several of her novels. The Salem to Lowell railroad came through North Reading in 1850 with a station where North Reading Auto now stands across from Emma's Classic Cuts. Did you ever wonder why that road is called Railroad Avenue?

Three of her novels, *The Right Princess, Jewel* and *Jewel Storybook,* proselytize her conversion to Christian Science. In 1894 when Mary

Baker Eddy spoke in Chicago, Clara attended a meeting for which her older bother, Fred, played the organ. Clara's first Christian Science book got her into some trouble with her publisher. Houghton Mifflin also owned *The Atlantic,* which had been lampooning Eddy and Christian Science. "The controversy died down when Houghton Mifflin substantially increased Burnham's royalties," says Mary Rubenstein.

How do Burnham's romances read today? Members of the North Reading book group, in general, felt the books are interesting period pieces and intriguing because of references to the Ipswich River and local haunts, but somewhat dated and predictable. "So much of the plot depended on coincidence," observes Pat Snedeker.

"They may have been good in their time," suspects Ann McDonnell, "but I prefer Thomas Hardy, Joseph Fielding, Thomas Mann. I am still trying to finish reading my classics."

Molly Leonard picked up the Burnham book set in San Diego's Coronado Hotel "because we had been there. It was slow going at the start, but then she introduced more characters. Now I plan to finish it."

Marilyn Henderson, chair of the book group, said, "Some of our members didn't think the books were very sophisticated. I read three, and they were pretty similar."

Other members of the book group, which began two and a half years ago, include Janet Comerford, Lois Waller, Ken Finch and Dr. Bill Meehl.

The book club meets the last Wednesday of each month in the Library Activity Room. Books for the coming year include Faulkner's *As I Lay Dying,* Thomas Wolff's *Look Homeward, Angel,* Sinclair Lewis's *Babbitt,* and James McBride's *Color of Water.*

The Rubensteins lived in North Reading only four years before the Navy shipped them off again to California and Chicago. "It's a strange thing," muses Ralph, "every place we moved in the Navy was linked to Clara Louise."

Mary recalls, "We returned to North Reading when Ralph retired in 1980 because we had all made good friends here. Some special bonds came from our early association with the North Reading Library book group when Marge Hill was library director."

And what does Mary Rubenstein plan to do with her collection of Clara Louis Burnham novels? "Eventually I will donate them all to the library. Clara is not on the level of Louisa May Alcott, but she is ours, and we should preserve her memory."

—September 4, 1998

Four

Hornet Pride and Art à la Carte

West Village School House, 1844

Arthur Kenney, Principal Emeritus

Principal of North Reading High School from 1965 to 1981, Arthur "Art" J. Kenney, divides his retirement now between his homes in North Reading and Littleton, New Hampshire. Robust and positive, Arthur Kenney often walks three miles a day with his North Reading neighbor, Warren Shaffer, around their Marshall Street neighborhood. The walking more of a challenge in New Hampshire, Art, in the last ten years, has trekked with his son David to all "the huts" except Madison in the Presidential Range of the White Mountains. Staying fit and keeping long established friendships vibrant are themes that run through this former principal's retirement years.

Art grew up in Milford, Massachusetts, playing sandlot baseball in the 1920s with friends like Bernie Marcus, "Tate" Bodio, Hank Camoli, Pete Stock, Hank Lutfy and Charlie Brucato. Many of these boys went on to careers in professional ball. Speaking of the mixed ethnicities these friends represented Art said, "It didn't matter who was on the playground. What we were looking for was ability."

A hard-throwing left-hander who also relied on his curve ball, Art pitched twenty wins in his Milford High career, fifteen wins with the "Legion" team he belonged to in high school, and sixteen wins at his college, Holy Cross.

He credits his Milford coach, Al "Hop" Riopel, with teaching him the basics.

"Coach Riopel took a group and whipped them into a team. He was interested in me." Coach Riopel having moved on to coach at Holy Cross in 1933, Art followed him to that institution with a president's scholarship in 1935.

During Art's years at Holy Cross, his college team played preseason exhibition games against the Red Sox in April when they came from spring training. Art pitched to Jimmy Foxx and struck him out twice. In 1938 Holy Cross beat the Sox 4-2.

"They were all close games," he said.

After earning his Holy Cross diploma, in June of 1938, Art signed a professional contract with a Boston Braves scout, getting $3,000 in bonuses and $1,000 per month. "That was a lot of money in those days," he said. Babe Ruth, who played his last year of professional ball with the Braves in 1935, made $80,000 at the height of his career. Some one commented to him, "You made more than the president of the United States"

"That's right," said Babe Ruth. "I had a better year, too."

Art's manager in 1938 was Casey Stengel, who went on to more successfully manage the New York Yankees and the Mets. In the summers of 1938 and 1939 the Braves farmed Art's pitching skills out to teams in Hartford and then Toronto.

"They sent me out for seasoning," he said. His promising cbaseball areer was cut short, however, by World War II. Joining the Army Air Air Corps, Art spent the next four years in the service, eighteen months of that time in England as a communications officer, attaining the rank of captain. As a member of the 398th Bomb Group and the 603rd Bomb Squadron, Art was part of the air echelon in charge of signals.

"If you saw the movie *Twelve O'clock High,*" he explained, "I was the officer at the pilots' morning briefing who explained what the flight crews needed to do to call for help. Each one got a 'flimsy,' a set of secret information printed on rice paper. They could eat those instructions if they got in trouble," he said.

Such was the camaraderie during the war that the 390th Bomb Group still exists sixty years later. They maintain a meeting room in Seattle, Washington, and publish a paper, *Flat News,* that arrives every month. The war over, Art went back to school at University of New Hampshire to get his master's degree. Next he taught briefly at Twin Mountain High School in the town of Carroll near Bretton Woods, where he subsequently was principal for four years. Some of his former students, in fact, own the Bretton Woods Corporation today, which includes The Bretton Arms, the Cog Railway, historic Mount Washington Hotel, and now the ski slope itself.

After Art served another twelve years as Littleton High School principal, a UNH classmate and friend, Dana Cotton, came for a visit. Dana was the director of the New England Association of Colleges and Secondary Schools at the time, and taught education courses at Harvard University.

"You should think about coming down to the Boston area to work," Dana suggested.

"I'm happy here," replied Art. But he also understood that it would be a good career move. Dana soon conveyed that he had spoken with a Dr. George Quinn, superintendent of schools in North Reading Massachusetts, who was looking for a high school principal. In January 1964, Art accepted the appointment and came to work here.

"When I came, Frank O'Donoghue was head of the English department. I had great respect for him. What a decent person and a good friend," remembered Art. Frank O'Donoghue soon left North Reading High School to become assistant superintendent in Reading. "In 1970, when Frank applied for North Reading's superintendent position, of course we endorsed him heavily," added Art.

Dr. O'Donoghue had also coached baseball and loved the game, remembers Mary Frances Sawyer, the secretary to the superintendent of schools since the 1970s. She recalls a picture Bob Turosz took of Dr. O'Donoghue, Arthur Kenney, and Bill Butler, the principal who succeeded him, watching a baseball game.

"They all shared the love of the game," said Mary Frances.

"In 1965 Mr. Kenney took a chance hiring me," said Frank Carey, North Reading High School's legendary baseball coach for the past thirty years. "There may have been better candidates out there, but he gave me the opportunity." With their mutual love of baseball, there could not have been a better match. Frank's father died during Frank's first year teaching. "Mr. Kenney is like a second father to me. He always treated kids and teachers with respect and dignity. No matter what happened in a tough game, he'd lift our spirits afterwards."

Peter Hill, North Reading High School class of 1970 and physical education teacher in North Reading since 1975, was a member of Frank Carey's first varsity team in 1968. "As principal of the school Mr. Kenney was an authority figure, not a buddy. It was a different era," said Peter. Students knew Art had pitched in the big leagues, but Peter and his teammates were surprised when their principal joined them one day out on the field for batting practice. "When we won our first state championship in 1969, there was Mr. Kenney in the parking lot carrying bats. I have a picture of him," said Peter.

Art used to fondly refer to Shirley Plouff, the high school office secretary, as The Commander. "Someone had to guard the gate," he said. During the twenty-two years Shirley sat at that desk, she recalled people coming to the school to get Art's autograph on baseball memorabilia. "Mr. Kenney was so constant; everybody loved him. But a rule was a rule. It didn't matter if it was my child or Nancy Norton's; he used the same standard of fairness. He was very formal on the outside, but not on the inside," said Shirley. "Arthur Kenney was a true gentleman."

"In all the years I've known him, I have never heard the man curse," observed Frank Carey. "Other people don't curse in his presence, either."

Art, not surprisingly, also has a high opinion of Coach Carey. "Frank taught discipline, respect and skills. His heart and soul were in the game of baseball. I'd watch the team in April and think, 'I don't know about this year.' A month later they would be a different team," said Art.

One of his greatest frustrations as principal was the public's lack of understanding and support of the 1970s "open campus" policy that was needed to alleviate overcrowding and avoid double sessions. Constructed to house 800 students, the high school building held, at the time, closer to 1,200. "People thought students spent too much time at Ryer's Store. My feeling was, if you want to teach kids responsibility you have to give them some. In my forty years in education, ninety-seven percent of the kids I knew were terrific. It is only a few who create problems." Admitting that he did, however, watch the parking lots closely, Art remembers calling the police once to question the presence of a scruffy looking character on the driveway between the Batchelder playground and the high school field, only to find out the man was an undercover detective.

Art appreciates having worked for some wonderful school committee members over the years. In his view, a good school board member asks good questions, sets policy, and holds its employees to carry out that policy.

"Bill Ryer was one of the best. He asked the most penetrating questions. Ester Zeimetz was one school committee member who actually visited the schools; she was very fair, very honest." Afraid to mention any for fear he would forget someone, Art also paid homage to Marty Connolly, Bob Mauceri, Bob Germino, and Eleanor Puglia. "Tom O'Leary was responsible for rebuilding the track properly. And don't forget Ralph Hudson—there was a man who also gave generously of his time," he said.

What were his greatest pleasures as high school principal? "I loved working with kids. Of course, I was interested in the athletics, but I loved the music groups, too; Harold Weiss had wonderful bands and shows. It was never a job for me to go to the kids' activities."

Art and his wife chaperoned almost all the dances and loved to dance. He recalls that Vice Principal Ed Baressi's wife, Greta, once was picked by mistake for the prom queen at a high school dance. A beautiful woman, she was, nonetheless, terribly embarrassed.

At the last of eighteen graduations Art attended, he got up to accept the class gift on behalf of the school as he always had. His wife, Lorraine, did not usually go to the graduation ceremony on the football field because seating was limited and families of the graduates needed to be accommodated first.

In 1981, however, she decided to attend, this being the last one. When the president of the senior class, Russell Bowers, unveiled a permanent sign that read ARTHUR J. KENNEY ATHLETIC FIELD, Art was totally taken aback.

"I couldn't believe it. I couldn't talk. It was the best-kept secret," he said.

"It *was* the best-kept secret," repeated Lorraine. "I felt sorry for Art—he almost fell apart."

—*February 4, 2000*

Frank Carey, Baseball Coach

You've seen them in their green T-shirts and green baseball caps as you come out of the post office or the bank, boys squinting in the sun, looking to catch the fly ball. Founded in 1980, North Reading Baseball School offers local youngsters the basics in hitting, batting, catching, throwing, pitching and sliding every summer. It also offers a few lessons in sportsmanship and hard work. Frank Carey, founder of this first baseball camp in eastern Massachusetts, came to North Reading in September 1965, hired to teach science. Two years later, when the varsity coach left for Brookline High School, Frank Carey became the North Reading varsity baseball coach, a position he has now held for thirty years. Pete Hill, Frank's codirector at the baseball academy, played for North Reading High School in 1969, Frank's first team to become state champions. But that was only the beginning.

North Reading High School baseball teams went on to win the Eastern Massachusetts finals four times, placed second in the state play-offs twice, and first in the state championship in 1969, 1970, 1974 and 1982. Frank's lifetime coaching record is 523–192. But the statistics do not tell the whole story.

Frank Carey always knew he wanted to work with kids. Brought up "Italian" in a tenement in Lynn, Frank studied the accordion until he was fifteen. "Playing the accordion was part of your heritage. You took lessons at the conservatory. My first accordion had twelve bass buttons, but later I had a Tony Constantino accordion with 120 buttons. Mother-of-pearl. The works. I kept telling my mother I wanted to play at Fenway Park, not Carnegie Hall. Frank remembers having two groups of friends when he was a kid: the motorcycle gang who later joined Hell's Angels, and the athletes. "I was loyal to both groups, and I was on the fence. I can relate to kids on the fence. Let's just say I was academically challenged, and I could have gone either way."

But there were role models. Coach Nipper Clancey at St. Mary's High School in Lynn, and Dr. Elmo Benedetto, athletic director for Lynn Public Schools, really pushed Frank to apply to college and helped him get the scholarships he needed to attend the University of Rhode Island.

Frank played football his first year at URI, but after an injury had to have his kneecap replaced. "That operation got me out of football." For two years he played baseball, but by his senior year he had married his sweetheart from Lynn; his first daughter was born just before his graduation.

"I had to work through school. I always worked summers. My first year at North Reading I earned $4,900. Took home seventy-seven dollars a week." In the summers Frank had to work construction, paint houses and load trailer-trucks at Sears. In 1980, he decided if he was going to work summers, it would be at what he loved. The first summer fifty boys came to the baseball school; the second year, 100. Today Frank runs his baseball academy two to three weeks in North Reading and one week in Lynn.

Are young people different today? Immediately Frank answers, "Yes." First they are not as respectful as he remembers. "But respect is a relative thing. If they don't listen to their parents, why does it surprise us that they do not listen to their teachers and coaches? I used to make sure kids on my teams stayed out of trouble. Now I tell parents 'I'll take care of your kids from eight to five, Monday to Friday. After 6:00 P.M. ... they are yours.'"

The other trend Frank notices is that kids today are less skilled. Why is that? "In 1968 no one had a computer, a swimming pool, a car, a TV. There are too many things for them to do now, and they don't have time to play ball. This is not necessarily a bad thing. Kids may have more training, more equipment, but they aren't down at the park or out on the street playing ball every chance they get."

Does he keep up with former players? "You bet. We've had an alumni game every year on Memorial Day since 1975." The Hunt Memorial game raises $250 to scholarship a senior player each year.

Frank also runs a baseball alumni golf game. Pat Lee, owner of the Horseshoe Café and star player from 1971–73, caters the tournament. Players donate prizes for a raffle. Over the years events like these have provided funds for two portable backstops, bat speed meters, three batting cages, two pitching machines and an electronic scoreboard. Just recently, while he was in San Diego at a baseball convention, Frank purchased a major league batting cage with money raised by alums, and at no cost to the town. Are there special memories? At the National College Baseball Coaching Convention some years ago Frank met baseball coaches from Curaçao, an island off the coast of Venezuela. In 1980, fifteen North Reading High School baseball team members traveled, expenses paid, to give clinics on this island near Aruba, and to play the inaugural game in Curaçao's National Baseball Stadium.

"We had to get permission from the U. S. Baseball Federation to represent the United States. We were on TV, exchanged gifts, and carried greetings from the U. S. Congress and Massachusetts' Governor King. It was a pretty big deal." The exchange was reciprocated the next year when the Curaçao coach's son, Hugo Daou, attended NRHS and lived with Peter Salem's family on Central Street.

At this point Frank interrupts our conversation, "Pitchers, hold up a sec. Look. Rocker step, tuck hold. Don't pivot on that heel, you'll end up on top of the rubber! Hold that tuck, then throw."

Turning again to the bleachers, "I don't expect kids to come out ready for Fenway Park, but they'll learn some basic skills."

—*July 17, 1998*

Agatha Marano, Drama Coach

Agatha Marano began teaching at North Reading Middle School in 1968. In 1970 she helped Linda Welsh with the choreography of *South Pacific*. While Linda was still directing, Agatha helped with the dancing, the scenery, the costumes, and the dialect coaching.

When did she begin dancing herself? Growing up in Swampscott, she took dance lessons in Lynn with Dorothy and Robert Canessa from the time she was three years old. Robert Canessa was the original "dream" Curly in the first national touring company of *Oklahoma*. "I was a hoofer, a tap dancer. There wasn't a Friday night we didn't put on our costumes and get on a bus to go to a nursing home or present a minstrel show," said Agatha.

And what was her directing background? "Zip. Zero," she said. "I came from the Linda Welsh School of Theatrical Knowledge."

Linda, an English teacher at North Reading High School since 1969, founded the original Masquers Club in the spring of 1970 with the help of student Leslie Waller. For the next six years Linda directed plays, Agatha sharing the work. "Agatha is a tremendously talented person. She may have learned a few things about blocking or creating a visual picture on stage from me, but I can't take all the credit." Agatha has also directed *Don't Drink the Water* at the University of Lowell, and *Come Blow Your Horn* for the Swampscott Theater Company.

What keeps Agatha Marano going? "I like to be busy. But I see young people come away from this with skills. ... Let me give you an example. Stephen Kazmierczak's mom told me that he recently stood in as the best man in a wedding because the real best man was ill. When asked to give the toast, they brought him a microphone. 'I won't be needing that,' he said, 'I know how to project my voice.' "

Many of Agatha's stars have gone on to use their acting, dancing or backstage skills in college or as adults. Carol O'Neill worked for Disney in the Electric Light Parade; Andrew Sawlar acted in Boston Shakespeare Company. Teresa O'Brien performed on cruise lines after graduating; Up with People recently selected Gwen Bourque in its international cast. Heather Wood worked at the Hart College Playhouse in Maine; Tom Kieran has done voiceovers in the Boston area. Tricia Zalewski opened her own dance studio in Ohio, and Lance Bourque pursued a professional career in ballet.

Currently the dance captain at North Shore Music Theater's *A Chorus Line,* and playing the part of Bobby, is North Reading's own John Fedele. Remembered for his evil Mordred in North Reading High School's *Camelot* in the early 1980s, Fedele has been in fourteen road companies of *A Chorus Line*. He has played Rooster Cogburn in road shows of *Annie* all over the world; last summer he danced in Lincoln Center's production of *Sweet Charity* with Gwen Verdon and Chita Rivera.

Agatha well remembers how John became a dancer in *Hello Dolly*. One of the kids had dropped out; she needed an additional dancer for the "Waiters' Gallop." Agatha instructed her assistant Fred Rice to go out of the auditorium and "pull in the next guy who walks down the hall." That young man, who had never danced before, was John.

"She is from the 'Do It, or Else' School of Theater," said Greg Kalafatos. "She's good."

—*November 20, 1998*

DiFranza Designs

Shortly after the move to the new library in 1991, head librarian Roz Spielman spoke to Happy and Steve DiFranza of DiFranza Designs, who live in the Edwin Foster House adjacent to Damon Tavern, about the possibility of creating a hooked rug for the library's front stairwell to add warmth, minimize echoes and be public art.

At the reception honoring the retiring Roz Spielman, North Reading residents had their first opportunity to view this fabulous gift to our town. Hanging in the library stairwell was a hooked rug, nine feet by five feet, depicting the historic Town Common: The Third Meeting House, bandstand, Putnam House, West Village School, Damon Tavern, Edwin Foster House, flagpole—even the mighty oak.

Steve DiFranza, a graduate of the Boston Museum School, graphic designer and painter, presented the library trustees with five or six designs from which they chose the Common scene. In 1993 Steve's wife, Happy, Smith College graduate in art history, began to cut her #6 wool strips of 6/32 of an inch and to hook the landscape she sees out her window past her manicured garden of peach poppies, black iris and honeysuckle vine.

Hooking began for Happy in 1960 when she took an adult education course at North Reading High School, taught by Ethel Bruce from Haverhill, a respected teacher of hooking with a wonderful color sense.

"We had moved to North Reading in 1959 and bought a little house on Elm Street. Our baby, Elizabeth, was born in 1960. In those days women were still at home, not so frazzled trying to manage job, home and children. We had an empty house with borrowed furniture. I thought we needed some rugs."

A year later, Happy brought a sketch of Steve's design for a nursery rug to class. Ethel Bruce later told Happy she was so excited by the project idea that she could not sleep that night, but she never thought this young mother would have the time to stick with it. Alice in Wonderland, the rug Happy made for Elizabeth, still hangs in the front hall on Bow Street. The white rabbit on a new Alice rug is now hooked for granddaughter Angela Rosa Petretta. Work on this rug will resume when the library rug is complete.

Making rugs by hand has a long history, but no example of hooked rugs as we know them today can be dated much before 1850s when Edward Sands Frost, a Maine tin peddler developed the commercial pattern. During the nineteenth century, floor coverings became increasingly fashionable and practical since carpeted floors relieved winter drafts. Burlap was widely available in flour or grain bags, and frugal housewives could use woolen scraps from old clothing or buy them at New England woolen mills by the pound. Dry goods stores, as well as by Montgomery Ward mail order, sold patterns "all marked out." Rug hooking became a popular pastime.

Patterns are available "all marked out" today from DiFranza Designs in the fifth edition of its illustrated catalogue. Happy teaches classes in her studio, formerly the Bide-a-Wee gift shop, which prior to 1972 stocked, among other items, Campfire and Bluebird supplies.

In the thirty-plus years since Ethel Brace's adult education class, Steve and Happy have designed and hooked rugs for Mystic Seaport, Beauport in Gloucester and *Good Housekeeping* magazine. This summer Happy will participate in a juried show at the Wenham Museum where her Noah's Ark rug for her grandson, Dominic, will be displayed.

In 1992, Stackpole Books published the DiFranza's *Hooking Fine Gifts* that led to a chapter in the British publication *Hooked Rugs* in 1995, featuring their designs "Bird on the Vine" and "Patchwork."

Commissioned hooked rugs generally run from $200 to $500 a square foot. At this price the rug depicting North Reading's Common is worth well over $10,000. The DiFranza's have donated five years of their professional time, skill and materials to this project and to our town.

At the end of our visit, Happy let me cut one #6 strip of green flannel wool in her wool-slitting machine. "I'll use these strips tomorrow morning to fill in more of the grass by the bandstand. Look over here at the border. This light spring green was a favorite suit of my mother's, and this gray in the stone wall was a favorite skirt of mine."

—*June 12, 1998*

Rozelin Spielman, Librarian

"We were unanimous after meeting her," recalls Diane Norris, chairwoman of the library board of trustees and voluntary member of that board for the last twenty-five years. "The search committee wondered how they could go through the process of interviewing the rest of the candidates; it was that unanimous. We had to be coy—say we would check her references, but we knew right away that Rozelin Spielman was perfect for us."

Graduating from Brandeis in that institution's second graduating class, with a degree in Hebrew literature, Roz decided to continue her education at Columbia where she earned a master's degree in library science. First-generation Polish immigrants, her parents had few opportunities for formal education but always encouraged their three children to stretch their minds. After high school Roz had the option of living at home and attending Brooklyn College essentially free. With Brandeis in its infancy, there was some question whether credits would even transfer back to Brooklyn College should Roz decide to come home. But Roz went off to Massachusetts.

Prior to their move to the North Shore of Boston, her husband had been the rabbi of a large temple in Randolph while Roz served as head librarian in the Hanover Public Library. Rabbi Spielman took a position at Temple Emmanuel in Wakefield fourteen years ago, at which time Roz applied for the North Reading Library position.

In October 1985 Roz moved into her corner office in what is now the refurbished Damon Tavern on Bow Street. In those days before electronic beepers, the first floor of the library had large tables on which the new town engineer, Ray Frazer, liked to spread out his blueprints and concentrate on his work away from his ringing phone. One morning Roz asked him if he would like a tour of this quirky, historic building.

"As an engineer, he was noticing different things than I had noticed." As Ray tried to run a single piece of paper between bookshelf and ceiling he commented, "Those beams are supported by the book shelving!" Within twenty-four hours structural engineers had agreed. The Weeks Building was condemned, and it closed in December 1985 just two months after Roz assumed her new position.

A temporary library of 2,000 items moved to share the North Reading High School Library space, and remained there until April 1986. During those months, workers installed steel lally columns to shore up the ceiling, and attempted to fix the leaking roof in the Weeks Building. In April the structural engineers gave temporary occupancy permits on the condition that most of the first-floor book storage move to the lower level in what had been the children's room. Temporary turned out to be a very long time. The trustees tried to sell the town on the efficiency of a combined town and high school library. The town voted this plan down in April 1985, and they voted it down again in April 1986. "We got the message."

At that time the Flint Building was vacant, the Town Hall having moved to the Murphy Center. After endless consideration of the feasibility of various locations, the board of trustees hired architect Max Ferro of the Preservation Partnership to convert the Flint Building to the North Reading public library. Ferro's offices in New Bedford were of the same period as the Flint Building, complete with mansard roof. Max, in fact, was the only architect interviewed who had a vision for this historic location.

In October 1991 more than 100 volunteers from North Reading moved the books across the street to their new library home. "That was one of my nightmares," remembers Roz. "What if the people who said they would help did not come? We started moving books on Thursday of Columbus Day Weekend, and by Sunday the task was finished." Individuals who carted books had a true sense of ownership. "That's my shelf," a library patron would say.

Mary Rubenstein, new library trustee and retired library staff member said, "We owe that beautiful building to Roz. Yes, she did battle for everybody. She wouldn't settle for second best. She put on her hard hat regularly and conferred daily with the clerk of the works. We owe her big. We really do."

We owe Roz for more than a new and beautiful library building. She has taken us from card catalogue days to eight stations of computers hooked to the Internet. She clearly remembers the days when "We used to have a rubber stamp with the date on it, and you signed your name after presenting your paper library card in its cardboard sleeve."

Diane Norris recalls the evening she and Roz worked feverishly on a presentation for town meeting to persuade citizens to support a tax override for the new library building. Each family's share would amount to the cost of merely one pizza per week. New to this technology, they struggled with the computer spread sheet. Roz's approach was, "I have to learn this. It is part of my job." Years later she served on the computer upgrade committee for Merrimack Valley Library Consortium (MVLC), an organization over which she recently presided.

Roz has always brought an absolute standard of professionalism to her job. She knows we are not the Boston Public Library, but her standards are no different. She is committed to meeting the needs of the community and of the reading public. When she arrived here there were few library policies for book purchase. Based on the American Library Association's "Freedom to Read" policy, she has been committed to the serious job public libraries have to supply uncensored information and make democracy work at its most grassroots level.

"As a trustee," remembers Dick Canterbury, "I found Roz to be thoroughly professional, always prepared, good-humored and above all, sensible."

As Roz and Bernard pack their Wakefield home this summer to move to their duplex in Del Ray Beach, Florida, our librarian of thirteen years leaves a legacy of quality and professionalism she assumed was commonplace. It will be a great challenge to find someone with her talents to succeed her.

—*June 19, 1998*

Lawrence Colford, Piano Technician

When Lawrence Colford returned from his two-year U. S. Navy tour of duty as an electrician on the USS *Hamner* DD 718, he was looking for a job. During World War II, piano production in this country had halted. Lawrence saw an ad in the newspaper placed by the Ivers and Pond Piano Company in Cambridge seeking piano craftsmen. "I liked the idea of being a craftsman," he recalls. "Tuning actually scared me."

Referred by the Veteran's Administration, Lawrence Colford signed up for a free nine-month course with the Henry L. Pierce School on Washington Street in Dorchester. The school housed a cooking tutorial as well as a program for aspiring piano technicians. A nine-month course, the piano program taught the basic principles: rough and fine-tuning, regulating, and voicing. There were six or seven in Lawrence's class. Some went on to specialize as stringers, finishers or tuners; most continued their studies as apprentices.

After a six-month apprenticeship at the Hallet and Davis Piano Company on Summer Street in Boston, Lawrence applied for a job at the Baldwin Piano Company.

"Piano tuning has never been that competitive a business," he said. "There is opportunity everywhere."

Debbie Cyr, a member of the faculty at the North Bennet Street School in Boston, confirms the high demand for piano technicians. Apprenticeships are difficult to find today; if you want to learn this trade, there are only two institutions with full-time programs: George Brown University in Toronto and the North Bennet Street School, said Debbie. Specializing in training for trades that use hand tools,

The North Bennet Street School has a waiting list for most of its programs, which include lock-smithing, preservation carpentry, jewelry making, violin and 'cello making and, of course, piano technology.

"You do not need to know how to play the piano or read music to be a piano technician," said Debbie. "There are no entrance exams. We teach you everything." For this one or two-year, hands-on program there are scholarships and grants available to cover the $10,000 per year price tag. "There is always a shortage. We can never produce enough graduates to fill the positions open all over the country," she said. Maybe this demand is one reason why Lawrence has a hard time retiring.

In his first years with Baldwin Piano Company, Lawrence went to homes to tune and adjust pianos that had been sold in Baldwin's Boston showroom. By the time he left Baldwin fourteen years later, he was the head technician, tuning the pianos for all Symphony Hall concerts when the artist used a Baldwin. Not only did he tune for many of the jazz greats such as George Shearing, Erroll Garner, and Oscar Peterson, he also tuned for classical musicians such as Jorge Bolet and the husband and wife duo Pierre Luboshutz and Genia Nemenoff.

The tuning business requires patience with the instrument, but is also demands patience and diplomatic skills with the client. "You have to be able to contend with all comers," said Lawrence. "I had prepared the pianos for Luboshutz and Nemenoff in Jordan Hall. When they arrived to practice, Ms. Nemenoff exclaimed 'Somebody washed these keys! Who washed these keys?' 'I never wash the keys,' I replied. Many concert pianists want the keys gritty." Lawrence once heard an old-timer from the Steinway Company confess he used hair spray to make the keys sticky. Lawrence, however, would not recommend it.

In his days with Baldwin, he tuned the personal pianos of Arthur Fiedler, Eric Leinsdorf and Leonard Bernstein's mother in Brookline. "Mr. Fiedler had three Baldwin pianos in his home: a spinet, a grand and a Hamilton upright. Mr. Leinsdorf had two grands in his living room: a Steinway and a Baldwin," remembered Lawrence.

Currently without a working piano in his own home in North Reading, Lawrence purchased a Steinway five years ago, which he is rebuilding in his studio. The cast-iron plate leans against the wall; the hammers with new felts sit on a closet shelf with numerous mothballs. The spruce sounding board has a few cracks that he is filling with matching wood.

"I take my time," he said. "Acme Piano in Somerville will refinish the mahogany case. Look at this wood grain!" The 6'1" grand will have all new strings; Lawrence orders them from the American Piano Supply in Clifton, New Jersey. Finished, this piano will sell in the $15,000 to $20,000 range.

This is not the first time Lawrence has found a treasure in someone's parlor. In 1980 a group of North Reading music lovers, including Katharine Barr, Happy and Steve DiFranza, Eleanor Puglia, Lucille Carberry and Beth Thomson, formed a committee to find a piano for the Weeks Building ballroom. The Flint Library was housed in the Weeks Building, and Beth Thomson had organized a very popular Rufus Porter Music Series in the upstairs room where there are priceless Rufus Porter murals and amazing acoustics.

The committee asked Lawrence to let them know if any of his clients were selling a piano appropriate for the library ballroom. In 1981, he found one. Lucille Carberry and Beth Thomson drove into Cambridge to see the 1893 American Steinway which belonged to an eighty-six-year-old woman who was not sure she wanted to sell her engagement present. After Lucille played Mozart, the owner decided she could part with the piano. Sometimes these transfers of musical instruments are more like adoptions than sales.

While fund-raising efforts for the ballroom piano had already begun, Charles Statuti, a North Reading lawyer who was in an East Boston nursing home at the time of the purchase, covered the balance so that the sale could proceed. Eventually more than seventy people paid $75 to buy a piano key. The piano, which now lives in the Flint Library Activities Room, has a brass plaque remembering those who gave to The Kitty for the Keys.

Beth credits the committee, Charles Statuti and Lawrence Colford for accomplishing the purchase of the Steinway. "Charles Statuti donated the money because, he said, his mother would never forgive him if he did not." Mrs. Statuti had sent her sons on the train from East Boston to New England Conservatory every week to study piano and violin. Neither boy pursued his music into adulthood. "Larry Colford educated and persuaded us as to the value of this instrument," remembered Beth. "He brought a treasure to this town."

Did Lawrence's parents, like Charles Statuti's mother encourage his musical proclivities? His mother played piano growing up in Halifax, Nova Scotia. His father was a down-east fiddler from County Halifax. With training only from his father, he loved to play jigs and reels. There was always music in Lawrence's home on Mineral Street in Reading. The only professional musician in the family, however, his sister Jean, recently retired from thirty-seven years as a violist in the Dallas Symphony.

As a boy, he did not play an instrument until he was shipped off to Nova Scotia in the fifth grade to attend St. Anne's College, a parochial boarding school, with his brother. In his first year there, the priest in charge of the band gave Larry a trombone, but his arms were too short to reach the low notes. "He saw I was having trouble and gave me a valve trombone. I played the trombone until I returned to Reading High School for the ninth grade."

Lawrence does not really play much piano. What will he play first when he completes the 1927 Steinway piano in his basement that is only a year older than he is? "I might play a few show tunes, swing tunes. I like Fats Waller stuff and 'After You've Gone.'"

His greater pleasure over the years has come from preparing pianos so that the artist and the audience can enjoy a performance. "There is great satisfaction in concert work, especially when the performer is pleased," said Lawrence.

—February 5, 1999

Scott Wheeler, Composer

Do you write music every day or do you wait for "Inspiration?" someone once asked American composer Aaron Copland. "I wait for inspiration, and I do it every morning," he replied. While most of the rest of us are sleeping, North Reading composer, Scott Wheeler, as Copland did before him, is up at 5:00 or 6:00 A.M. Cup of tea in hand, Scott sketches out the next movement of his commission for the Toledo Symphony, his *Suite* for the New England String Ensemble or the overture to his new opera *Democracy*.

Scott has been writing music for twenty-five years. His first publishing success was a choral piece he sent out in 1980. "I got almost an immediate response. I was twenty-eight. I had to hand copy and photocopy everything at the time." Because he knew any computer program would be clearer than his "chicken scratch," Scott purchased Professional Composer in 1986 and subsequently switched to Finale in 1988, a program he still uses in his composing studio. The initial process, however, does not happen for Scott Wheeler in front of the MIDI or the computer screen—it still happens on staff paper, from his head, in the early hours of the day.

Born in Washington, D.C., Scott lived in St. Louis, upstate New York, Chicago, and Connecticut as a child. Because his father worked for IBM, which the family dubbed "I've Been Moved," Scott never attended an elementary school for more than two years.

"It didn't seem horrible at the time, but in retrospect I felt my siblings were fortunate to live in Darien, Connecticut, all of their childhood." Scott began piano lessons in the second grade. Then the family moved, and it was not until he was twelve that he had more lessons. "Then I dropped it," he recalled. "I discovered I could pick things up off the radio. I loved jazz, rock and show tunes."

In high school he and his friends formed a rock band called The Sleepless Knights. On a Farfisa keyboard, "cheesier" than a Hammond, Scott played blue-eyed soul. "I was a Beatles fan myself, but that was more sophisticated than the guys I was with. I did back up for 'My Girl,' that kind of thing." Scott's most important role in the band was to show his pals what chords to play.

Scott's parents enjoyed music; his father was a choir tenor and his mother, Dorothy Anastopolous, sang American pop songs on Greek radio during World War II. With sophisticated jazz tastes, she introduced him to Thelonious Monk, Dave Brubeck and Frank Sinatra.

"I know every note of these '60s records, but classical music was never in the house. I had two LPs: one of Wagner overtures and the other Prokofiev's *Classical Symphony,* and that was it," he said.

After studying premed at Amherst College for two years, music just sort of took over," recalled Scott. At the time his parents were not pleased that his college piano teacher, Monica Jukuc, and his composition teacher, Lewis Spratlan, had been so successful inspiring and instructing their oldest son. A 1973 Amherst College graduate, Scott went on to New England Conservatory for a year and then, with full scholarship, to earn his doctorate in music composition at Brandeis in 1984. While working for his doctorate, he also began his first teaching job at Emerson College. Part of the theater department, he was Emerson's only full-time music instructor, a position he still holds.

"Any composer needs a teaching job, but teaching has also been great fun! I have just conducted Bernstein's *Candide* this spring at the Emerson Majestic. The job has given me years of experience on stage, working with music in dramatic situations, and with more general audiences," said Scott.

A more elite audience would likely patronize the concerts of Dinosaur Annex, a musical organization dedicated to presenting work of living composers. The brainchild twenty-five years ago of composer Rodney Lister, mentor Ezra Sims, and Scott, himself, Dinosaur Annex took its name from a now-defunct dance company that helped the composers win nonprofit status. In the early years Dinosaur Annex gave seven to nine concerts a year. "We had puppy dog energy then," said Scott. "We've mellowed." With three concerts scheduled this season, Dinosaur Annex most frequently performs at First and Second Church, 66 Marlborough Street. They also have performed at First Night.

At First Night 1996, Scott Wheeler's *Piano Trio No. 2* premiered as part of First Works. It is this composition, which, The Gramercy Trio will record for CRI, and which was performed at Lincoln Center in New York City on March 3 and March 6, 2000. In January 1999, the *New York Times* announced Scott Wheeler had been awarded the 1999 Elise L. Stoeger Prize, a $10,000 cash prize given annually by the Chamber Music Society of Lincoln Center to two living composers "in recognition of significant contributions to the chamber music repertory." This prestigious award is not something for which one applies.

"I assume they knew of me because of my piece *Shadow Bands,* that was performed at Lincoln Center in May 1998. The players gave a great performance," he said. Part of the Lincoln Center Music of Our Time Series, the March 2000 concerts have repertoire from several centuries. "I love being on programs with Beethoven. The audience of standard repertoire are most willing to attend a musical train of thought for more than three minutes. I picked up on this classical tradition a little late, myself. I remember sitting through Rossini's *Barber of Seville* in my twenties, eyes on my watch. But if you want to know something about the human voice or about drama, Rossini has much to teach. Verdi is my current idol," said Scott.

For four or five years Scott wrote reviews of twentieth-century classical and Broadway CDs for *Fanfare* magazine and the *Boston Phoenix*. To make more time for the writing of music, he has stopped writing prose, except for recent entries in *The New Groves Dictionary of Music and Musicians*.

Last July, however, when his two daughters, Margaret, thirteen, and Lizzy, eight, wanted to see the rock group Hanson at Great Woods, Dad made an exception and reviewed the concert, including his daughters' opinions. Married to Christen Frothingham, an Episcopal priest at the Church of Our Saviour in Brookline, Scott has a tradition of composing valentines each year for the three women in his life.

"I try to write forty-five minutes to an hour of concert music per year. I also like to write pieces for special occasions. If I have been away from writing for a few months, the struggle to get back is painful; I write best when I write more. At one hour per year, I am relatively prolific," said Scott. A list of Scott's published and commissioned works, however, fills four pages. His styles and forms run the gamut from lullabies to rags, from symphonies to string quartets. One commission, *Fables*, was performed at Longy School in Cambridge on June 13, 1999, by flautist Julia Scolnik.

To complete some of these commissions, Scott has applied for and won fellowships to artist colonies where he might go for a month or three months at a time to compose. Last year he took up residence at the MacDowell Colony in Peterborough, New Hampshire, and at Yaddo in Saratoga Springs, New York, for part of his sabbatical from Emerson.

"I've applied to MacDowell again. I get so much done there. The little things that take up your time like appointments to get the oil changed in the car or trips to the dentist with the children, do not distract there. They give you a room with a piano and a fireplace. Lunch is delivered, and no one interrupts you all day. At the evening meal you chat with other visual artists, writers and composers,.

"We live in a business culture. To some, art is quite frivolous, and artists are considered parasites. At these retreats, poets are so relieved to see that what they do is valued," he said.

There is no doubt that Scott's work is highly valued and respected today. In his 1997 book *American Music of the Twentieth Century*, Kyle Gann said, "Scott Wheeler is a rare Virgil Thomson protégé ... he also studied ... privately with Peter Maxwell Davies. His music which started in a rather complex twelve-tone-derived idiom, has gone in the direction of ... neoclassicism. It has a sense of reserve ... expressive on a modest scale, never an overblown romantic style ... Wheeler's overriding aim has been to achieve an operatic idiom that learns from Broadway's clear sense of theater. So far this aim has found its largest expression in his large lyric cantata, *The Construction of Boston* (1988), a neoclassic work complete with harpsichord and banjo."

Josiah Fisk, in reviewing *Dragon Mountain* for the *Boston Herald,* called Scott's music "energetic, approachable, full-textured, optimistic."

Poet and winner of the Pulitzer prize for Music Criticism, Lloyd Schwartz commented in the *Boston Phoenix,* "Wheeler is not large-scaled and cosmic in the tradition of Mahler. He's rather a disciple of Virgil Thomson (literally) and even Stephen Sondheim—his works are appealingly modest, witty, elegant and tuneful. Very American, spiked with a splash of French vermouth and a lemon twist."

Does Scott customarily take the weekend off? "No," he said. "I write seven days a week. It is my greatest pleasure. Christen has tried to teach me to take a vacation. I am an avid tennis player. But mostly I feel hungry to get back to the writing."

—*June 7, 1999*

Marie Stultz, the Treble Chorus of New England

In the preface of her new book Marie Stultz quotes Picasso, "Every child is an artist until some adult convinces him otherwise." Composer, conductor and now author of *Innocent Sounds: Building Choral Tone and Artistry in Your Children's Choir,* North Reading's Marie Stultz has always respected the artistry in children. Rolling off the presses in January of 1999, her book makes its debut at the national convention of the American Choral Directors' Association in Chicago in late February. Will Marie be there?

"Is the sky blue?" Marie asks with a smile. "I already have the plane tickets."

She began working on the book in 1990 when she purchased her first computer. First planned as a seven-volume guide, Oxford Press wanted to call it *Training Your Children's Choir,* a scholarly title that Marie thought was terribly dry.

After holding the book for three years and three months, Oxford decided not to publish it. "Instead of being devastated, I decided I was just going to make this happen," she said. Soon afterwards, Rod Schrank and Ruth Lewis of Morning Star Music Publishers in St. Louis accepted it for publication.

"The book deals with the concept of pedagogy—what one does to build a children's choir from voice tone building to choosing a piece of choral music," said Marie. For example, Anthony Foster's "Betty Botter's Butter" is a great diction builder.

"Children can be taught to realize that their vocal potential and artistic abilities are limitless, that everyone can support, project and sing artistically with a beautiful tone," begins the second chapter of the book. In this chapter Stultz details the four "I's" of singing pedagogy: Intelligence, Imitation, Imaging, and Inner discipline.

Not only a resource for choral directors in church, school, or community, *Innocent Sounds* may also be used as a teaching textbook for college students interested in training children to sing, or as a guideline for department chairpersons as they develop their plans for music education curricula. A practical guide, *Innocent Sounds* is based on Marie's twenty-four years' experience directing the Treble Chorus of New England; prior to that she taught in public schools in Hamilton, Kansas, Wilmington, Massachusetts, and Burlington, Massachusetts.

"My first year teaching, I directed the marching band in Hamilton. We were proud of our moving diamonds going right down the field." Having come to associate Marie with Fauré, Vivaldi and Purcell, the marching band comes as a surprise.

Marie's marching band days began in Iola High School, Iola, Kansas, a town of 7,000 that produced a band of 115! Marie played flute in that band, which took her on a train to the Orange Bowl Parade, where the band received a standing ovation.

"Excellence is the most important factor in making music with children. I first learned this important lesson from my band director Dale Crietz," Marie remembers. Behind the grand piano he had a sign that said THINK. Dale also directed the orchestra in Iola, and introduced his students to quality classical music. Another early mentor and grade-school teacher, Irene Carrie, introduced Marie to the beauty of classical music through a performance of Handel's *Messiah*. Irene picked Marie, at the impressionable age of eleven, to be one of a select group singing the soprano arias. "We got to wear white collars; it really was quite special," remembers Marie.

Marie thinks that all too often students are deprived of high standards, being entertained rather than treated as promising artists. "Humankind has an innate need to sing. It would be impossible to count the number of times boys have been told that it is 'sissy' to sing, that making music deprives them of their masculinity. What if Leonardo da Vinci or Michelangelo had been told it was unmasculine to draw, to think or to create?"

Her teaching experiences have proven to her that students respond enthusiastically to high expectations, expectations that produce astonishing results. "That is what this book is about: high expectations of students through the medium of singing," she says.

As founder and artistic director of the Treble Chorus of New England, Marie has seen her dream of a professional caliber children's choir grow from infancy to artistic maturity. The choir has performed at St. Martin-in-the-Fields in London, with the Toronto Children's Choir in Canada, in Paramount Pictures' *School Ties;* they also have recorded three compact disks. In 1996 the TCNE traveled to Germany for exchange concerts with the Dresden Philharmonic Kinderchor and a music school in Leipzig. David Bailey went on that adventure. "We stayed with students who were my age in both cities. Musically it was absolutely great. The boat trip down the Elbe was also very cool."

In the fall of 1999, Marie conducts an *Innocent Sounds of Autumn* workshop at Otterbein College near Columbus, Ohio. Planned as a yearly event, in 2000 Otterbein will host a national conducting symposium, *Innocent Sounds of Summer*. Her hope is to participate in similar workshops for choral conductors across the United States and abroad, presenting the ideas in her book.

"The earlier you expose children to good music, to hearing and performing the most beautiful music of our cultural heritage, the more good music becomes part of their total artistic lives. I believe I was put on this earth to change the course of music education in this country," says Marie.

—December 18, 1998

Pearl Feeney-Grater, GraphoAnalyst

"I was probably the only student in the first grade of Immaculate Conception School in Winchester who had to stay after school because of my handwriting." When Sister Mary Louise asked Pearl Ann Feeney (now Pearl Feeney-Grater) to stay to practice the Palmer Handwriting Method on the blackboard, Pearl at first thought this was a special privilege. Even then she wondered, however, why her letters were not even or round, and why the strokes were not uniformly slanted. Pearl's mother consoled her by planting the idea that one day she might study the meaning of handwriting as her Great Aunt Sylvia in Canada had.

After graduating from Boston College with a degree in speech pathology and audiology and a minor in elementary education, Pearl earned her master's degree in speech and language at Boston University. For ten years she was a speech pathologist in the Waltham Public School System and taught graduate courses at Boston State College. "There was always a piece missing for me," she remembers. She did not feel speech could be separated from personality; she was always intrigued by the nonverbal side of language acquisition.

Remembering her mother's reference to Aunt Sylvia, Pearl started her research into handwriting. Her reading soon led her from pop literature to the International GraphoAnalysis Society in Chicago that, for a few thousand dollars, offers an eighteen-month correspondence course leading to certification in graphoanalysis.

By 1985 Pearl had passed her graphoanalysis exams, taken a leave of absence from her Waltham teaching position, and was working full time for a company in Wilmington with four certified associates. Although one graphoanalyist was an expert in court forgeries, this company primarily offered handwriting analysis services to the business community. Both small and Fortune 100 businesses hired Pearl and her associates to analyze personality for the purpose of team building, conflict resolution, hiring profiles and out-placement for departing employees.

Then along came a challenge to use her handwriting analysis skills in the business world for herself. In 1990 Pearl became the district manager for NovaCare, hiring, training, team building and providing customer service for twelve facilities in the Boston area. A number of years later she came full circle and returned to the public school setting where she had begun her career, this time as a speech pathologist for North Reading Public Schools.

"If you want to get your ideas supported in the work place, you need to understand your own working style; you also need to understand that others think differently and have contrasting styles." There are other tools out there, Myers-Briggs, for example, to determine what makes us tick, but in one three-hour session, a graphoanalyst, looking at only one half page of your writing and your signature, can identify over 300 personality traits.

The study of handwriting in Western societies dates to 1622 when an Italian philosophy professor wrote a book on the subject. Abbe Michon, a French priest, coined the term "graphology" in 1868, crafting the first system of handwriting analysis. At the turn of the century another pioneering French writer, Jules Crepieus-Jamin, published *A. B. C. of Graphology*. Germans and Swiss share the French fascination with graphology.

In Europe, in fact, up to eighty-five percent of companies employ a graphologist or graphology service to screen their job applicants. In the United States there is still skepticism; the figure is more like seven percent for businesses that admit to using graphology services, but this number is growing.

While Pearl's early graphoanalysis work focused heavily on the needs of the business world, her new company makes graphoanalysis more accessible to the average person. Founded eight years ago with Pat Carter of Lynnfield, Carter and Grater, Inc. still works with many business clients. A new subsidiary, SignOn, is on-line at Pearl's new Web site and available to all. For the private client, consultations are tailored to the needs and pocket book of the individual. You do not even need to leave your house for these services. Clients may fax a handwriting sample and discuss the result in a taped phone conversation, or have a face-to-face session of up to three hours.

And who might be interested in such services? Anyone who wants to understand a spouse, a boss, a child, a friend, a student, a fiancé. The August 1993 issue of *Bridal Guide* interviewed Pearl, suggesting that good communication is the key to a successful marriage, and "with a little help from a graphologist, the writing's on the wall." By understanding one's own personality traits, a bride, a spouse, an employee can begin to understand what kind of impact they are making and how they are being perceived.

"When people find out I am a handwriting analyst they say 'for you I will type.' People are afraid they will be found out or judged or criticized. I ask them, 'Is it better to have brown eyes or blue eyes? Be tall or short?' Personality traits are neutral. You are who you are." Handwriting analysis can help identify traits so that someone can develop strategies for dealing with people in his or her life who have opposite traits.

"As graphoanalysts we never say to marry this person, or not marry this person. Hire, or not hire this individual. We can tell you, however, in what areas you are compatible, and what will drive you nuts when working with this person."

In France, Germany and Sweden, medical doctors work closely with handwriting analysts. Research has shown health changes are often apparent in handwriting three to nine months before disease presents itself symptomatically. This medical aspect is an area to which Pearl has paid close attention over many years.

Some years ago parents of a young person, who had just broken off with her boyfriend, presented Pearl with a sample of their child's writing. Friends had told the parents she was suicidal. "I don't want to be asked these questions. I saw stress; I saw depression; I saw a need for support. The family had a red flag on what they suspected already, and a confirmation that propelled them to get professional help."

Another individual had suffered cancer and later came with a writing sample. He had been treated and considered himself cured. Pearl suspected a different outcome, "But he didn't ask me, and I didn't say."

Would every graphoanalyst see these matters of health in the handwriting? "No," says Pearl, "and there are many things I see in writing that I consider none of my business, but changes in health as reflected in writing has interested me for years." A number of years ago, Pearl suspected that there was a correlation between certain strokes in handwriting and stuttering. She wondered if by changing the writing stroke, the propensity to stutter might be less. While she has not had an opportunity to pursue this remedy in depth, she can, without question, identify stuttering in a client.

As we continued the interview I began to cover my writing. What was Pearl seeing in my scrawl? "It doesn't matter that it is upside down. I never read the content, just the strokes. And guess what? You already know yourself." She sees flexibility, intuition, ambition (this sounds good), but also a tendency to draw heavily from the past and a sensitivity to criticism. She assures me that traits are usually a blessing and a curse, but I am not altogether convinced they are neutral.

Skepticism, says Pearl, is common until people try handwriting analysis. "But the biggest skeptics fall the hardest."

—July 31, 1998

Five

Love in Action

The Third Meeting House, 1829

St. Theresa Volunteers at Camp Fatima

Four years ago John Silvestro invited Father Paul Ring, priest at St. Theresa's North Reading parish, to a visitor's day at Camp Fatima. Less than two hours from North Reading, Father Ring fell in love with these 150 acres on Upper Suncook Lake in Gilmanton Iron Works, New Hampshire. The following August, Father Ring was a volunteer at Camp Fatima's Exceptional Citizens (E. C.) week.

"I thought it might be a good way to give of myself," explained Father Ring, "but I got so much more than I gave. The campers' love knows no bounds. You walk away from that week feeling so uplifted. It's the highlight of my year."

E. C. Week is a nonsectarian, outdoor camping experience sponsored by the Roman Catholic Diocese of Manchester, New Hampshire. In its nearly forty years of operation E. C. Week has made a dream come true for more than 2,900 campers who are mentally or physically disabled. For 140 campers, this third week in August is a highlight in their lives; for their caregivers it may be the only week in fifty-two that they are not on call twenty-four hours a day.

While a contingent of ten to twenty-five North Reading residents have been volunteering at Camp Fatima E. C. Week for twenty years, this special week for exceptional children and adults actually began in 1954. Bill Haller, father of a Down's syndrome child, Tom Walker, a pediatrician at St. Paul's School, and Rev. Richard O. Boner, Associate Pastor at St. John's Parish in Concord, New Hampshire, had a dream in the early 1950s that exceptional children might have a camping experience like other kids. Teaming up with student nurses from Sacred Heart Hospital, Sisters of Mercy and Sisters of St. Francis, the founders' goal was to provide a fun and rewarding camp experience for twenty-five developmentally disabled young people.

Since that first year, Camp Fatima E. C. Week has grown to provide swimming, horseback riding and arts and crafts for 140 campers during the third week of August after the regular Camp Fatima boys camp has finished its season. Since E. C. Week is staffed entirely by 260 volunteers, a camper's enrollment is entirely free. Events throughout the year help raise more than $50,000, which covers among other things, the cost of feeding 400 volunteers and campers.

As a member of "head staff" for E. C. Week, former North Reading Selectwoman Nancy Cirone meets with other volunteers throughout the year to work on fund-raisers, and then serves as director of the recreation hall during camp week. "One of my many joys is seeing the families get free time," said Nancy. For some families it may be difficult to leave their exceptional young person in the care of strangers, as much as they might need a break. But by the end of the week there are "miles of smiles;" campers and staff have experienced "Love in Action," one of the camp mottos.

Heather and Tony LoRe have been volunteering at E. C. Week for thirteen and fifteen years, respectively. "John Unni invited us up for visitor's day," remembered Heather, "and my husband has been a counselor ever since." LoRe worked in the infirmary as a nurse practitioner at first; now she facilitates arts and crafts projects. LoRe described the structured day: three meals a day are mandatory, as is the quiet hour after lunch and daily mass held in various outside locations and celebrated over the years not only by various New Hampshire bishops, but also by Cardinals Cushing, Medeiros and Law. On visitors' day the bishop from Manchester traditionally arrives by helicopter.

North Reading resident Kristen Landry has attended E. C. Week as a camper four times, the first time when she was eight years old. She still remembers the magic of *Snow White* the first year she went. Her third summer at camp, Father John

Unni, who also grew up in North Reading, invited Kristen, who could now read, to offer one of the Bible readings at mass. This was a special honor for her.

Each camper has a counselor buddy who is responsible for his or her care twenty-four hours a day. Linda Barrasso, a counselor this summer at E. C. Week for her third year said, "The camper can't be left alone for a second. You sleep in the bunk above them, you have to wash them, dress them, and change their diapers. There are relief counselors to help if you need a break. You really have to like kids and like people. It's hard work, but we also have great fun. I love to do it."

Evening activities for campers and staff revolve around a different theme each year. Summer 1998's theme was *The Sound of Music*. Each evening the staff presents a one-hour portion of the production. Buffy Dysart Raymill will be volunteering this August to assist in the theatrical part of E. C. Week—*Oliver*.

Fun takes the form of costume parades, talent shows and dances; DJ Jim Plunkett regularly donates his time. The U. S. Marching Band makes an appearance, as do donated carnival rides from various New England vendors.

Adrienne Quercia, who talked her friend Linda Barrasso into trying E. C. Week, heard about Fatima eight or nine years ago from Father Unni and Tony LoRe. "I can't wait to go," she said. "It's hard work, but so much fun. When you see these counselors ... these young guys changing diapers ... being so gentle ... it is great to have a story about teens doing good things."

Father Jim Nyhan at Bishop Fenwick School convinced Andrew Kay to become a waiter at Camp Fatima E. C. Week when he was a high school sophomore. Andrew's brother Tim decided to go also. That was eight years ago; the brothers have not missed a summer since. Five years ago their parents, Dennis and Helen Kay joined them as did their sisters Emily and Elizabeth who helped for two years each. Three of their five years Helen and Dennis did all the camp laundry, often filling thirty machines at the Gilmanton Iron Works laundromat. "There is so much good in all of us," said Helen. "And the campers bring that out."

"It's a magic place," said John Silvestro. In the early 1980s, Silvestro's son, Paul, volunteered at E. C. Week with many of his North Reading friends. Many of them still meet on Thursday nights at Picadilly Pub to stay in touch with one another. Steve Sacco, Chuck Carrucci Jr., Jamie Ascenzo, Joey and Paul Unni (younger brothers of Father John) are all North Reading young people, who have given a week of their summer to serve as waiters or counselors at Fatima E. C. Week over the years. Kenny Parks even met his wife there.

John Silvestro did not become involved himself until the summer after his son, Paul's untimely death. Friends made donations to Camp Fatima in Paul's memory; it was that next summer that John Silvestro applied to be a counselor.

Campers and counselors complete a detailed questionnaire months before they arrive at camp, then are matched based on their various skills and limitations. A camper may need a counselor who is fluent in sign language, for example, or a counselor with a bad back may not be capable of lifting an adult camper.

Last summer John's camper, David, was severely autistic and did not speak. "What am I going to do with him for a week?" John remembers wondering. David was happy to splash in the lake and liked rides in the pontoon boat, but the biggest surprise, especially for David's parents, was the horseback riding. In spite of David's acute fear of animals, sitting on that gentle horse and walking around the ring with five counselors monitoring every step, was a highlight of his week.

"There is nothing fancy about the accommodations at camp," explained John. "There are usually twenty to a cabin, very Spartan conditions, bring your own sleeping bag. It is emotionally very intense—like having a baby all day long. I still feel a part of my son is there."

In 1997 Camp Fatima planted a tree in Paul Silvestro's memory. After learning the reason for the memorial, one of the campers went to the arts and crafts cabin and came out with a card for John, a heart scripted in glitter. "Love in Action," for sure.

"For some people this is their only week of vacation," said Father Ring. "I get four weeks, but even if I only had one, I think I'd still spend it here. These campers are maybe the closest things we have to love on earth."

—*June 28, 1999*

Joe Sadlow, Clerk of the Works at Church Renovation

In grammar school in Queens, New York, Joe Sadlow won the shop medal for an inlaid checkerboard he made. "Woodworking has been my hobby since I was six years old," he explains. "My father would lock up his shop, but I would pry the eyebolts open so I could slip off the lock."

Putting his carpentry skills to work for the past year, Joe has been the "clerk of the works" for the renovation project at Union Congregational Church on Haverhill Street in North Reading.

A member of the church since 1955 when he and his wife, Alice, moved to North Reading from Brooklyn, New York, Joe has long been one of the church's unofficial carpenters. He has made doll houses, toys and puzzles for the wood table at Frosty's Fair, repaired broken pews, designed and built a lazy Susan rack to hold the name tags of members, and installed wooden holders for pew Bibles.

Joe joined the Navy right after he graduated from Brooklyn Technical High School in 1942, having distinguished himself on the track and gymnastic teams there. He served in the Pacific on the USS *Fremont* during World War II, but never got struck by bullets or shrapnel. So it was quite ironic to return unscathed from the war and then to contract polio at the age of twenty-nine. "It was quite a shock. But it hasn't hampered me. Slowed me down a bit. You kind of forget."

The cane Joe uses has a wooden head he created. Inlaid with rosewood, cocobolo, mahogany and maple, it is the Masonic lodge insignia. He has been a Mason since 1956, and was a past master of the North Reading Lodge in 1984.

A mechanical engineer and professional model maker, Joe moved to North Reading because of a job with National Radio Company, a business that no longer exists. He retired from

Textron in 1990, but continues to build prototypes for industry. "It is a varied diet. One day you might build a model of a fire extinguisher, the next might be for a toy or a machine."

Gordon Hall, who worked with Joe on the church building committee, says, "I bet Joe made four or five models [of the new church space] as we changed things. He kept everyone's spirits up. No matter how discouraging our meetings were, Joe would always get up, push his chair back and say, 'Well, we're getting there.' "

Gordon saw issues of space, handicapped accessibility and plant upgrade as major reasons for the renovation. When there were overflow crowds, the congregation previously had to be split on two sides of the altar. Storage was also an issue. Handicap ramps had too steep a pitch to meet modern codes, and the steam heat was inefficient at best. The building now has hot water baseboard heat throughout.

The Reverend Richard Hughes praises all the church members who have come forward with expertise in various areas and helped with the project. "I have no experience in construction," admits Reverend Hughes. "This was far more complicated than I expected. It was hard to meet all the codes, and the codes often increased the cost." The handicapped lift from the sanctuary floor to the chancel area is hidden by a portion of the George F. Root choir stall wall, which Joe and Gary Rodgers recycled to this purpose. Only one wall of the original was needed to house the choir.

Nancy Parsons, chairperson of the Bricks and Mortar committee, a group, which now almost eight years ago raised money for the first architect's plans and the feasibility study, recalls a time prior to renovation when the handicapped accessibility to the altar area would have been put to good use.

"At Elva Pawle's ordination there was a laying on of hands, a blessing. Elva's father, an Episcopal priest and very elderly gentleman, was in a wheelchair. ... In the present chancel it could have been gracefully done," says Nancy.

After the members of the congregation voted in favor of the renovation project last March, Bricks and Mortar dissolved into two groups: one was the capital fund-raising arm, "Many Gifts, One Spirit," chaired by Nancy, and the other was the building committee chaired by Joe and Gordon. From that committee, Joe and Bob Messinger agreed to interface with the builders. "Joe was on the job, unpaid, just about every day," recalls Nancy. "He managed it. I can't think how."

For Nancy, the space and aesthetics of the worship area were of primary concern. Prior to renovation, altar space was limited, especially at weddings. Nancy recalled that retired minister, Reverend Harold Fohlin, once actually backed into the unity candle at a crowded wedding and lit his liturgical robes on fire. The best man beat out the flames, and the ceremony continued.

While changes are dramatic on the inside, the outside of the church has been altered little. There is a new entrance in Greek revival style, and there will be a small brass-roofed cupola on top of it. "Even though we held back from joining the historic district a few years ago because we expected there would be changes, we were careful to keep the exterior as close to the original as possible," says Nancy.

John Anderson with Dietz and Company in Springfield, Massachusetts, has been the head architect on the project, and Rico Colangeli of E. A. Colangeli Construction Company in Medford, the builder. Church members providing professional expertise and hands-on work, however, have helped and continue to help to keep the $600,000 price tag from going higher.

"The congregation was incredibly patient," says Reverend Hughes. "Nineteen to twenty-one weeks was the estimate for construction. It ended up taking nine months."

Demolition began the day after Easter 2000 and was completed, primarily by parishioners with sledge hammers and pickaxes. Member Ned Larkin installed the new heating in the sanctuary, while Arthur Pickett donated the heat for the new office and nursery portion of the building.

"Countless people did painting, moving and demolition," remembers Reverend Hughes. "Doug Lane, a sound engineer for the Red Sox and the Patriots, put in the sound system. One thing I've learned ... we all learned, was that we were building much more than a new sanctuary. We were building a stronger church community."

This church community began in June of 1720 when thirty-nine members called the Reverend Daniel Putnam to be the first settled pastor of the North Parish Congregational Church. Services were held in the First Meeting House, which was situated on the Town Common. The town built a second meeting house on the same site in 1752. In 1829, the Third Meeting House, also referred to as the Building on the Common, housed Congregationalists who by now had been joined by a more liberal thinking group of Universalists. A vote in 1832 for the parish to devote thirty Sundays each year to orthodox preaching and twenty-two to liberal sermons, did not resolve their growing differences. So in 1836 the more orthodox members split away and built a new worship space on Haverhill Street.

"From the columns forward is the oldest section, built in 1836," explains Joe. The walls have been refurbished with Navaho white and the door paint is sailcloth. New pews given by a church in Oxford, Massachusetts, which no longer has need of them, augment the curved oak benches which seat only 200, the new capacity being closer to 280. The carved oak benches replaced the boxed pews in 1896, according to an article written by Nancy Stewart, church historian, in the booklet that commemorates the church's 275th anniversary. In 1900 the church installed a pipe organ and moved the choir to the front of the sanctuary.

For Joe, one of the greatest challenges in this project was selling the idea of the two columns, which stand about where the exterior wall of the 1836 structure originally stood. Because of these weight-bearing columns, there are a few obstructed view seats. It would have been possible to remove these supporting pillars, but only at great expense. Over all, "everyone seems to appreciate the final design," he says.

Soon construction will start on the "Path of Remembrance," an outdoor meditation garden with a dogwood tree, benches, and over 160 inscribed bricks, a project headed by Jean Mascola and Nancy Parsons.

At the December 17, 2000, service, the first to be held in the new sanctuary, Nancy and Jean thanked Joe for the endless hours he has given to the church renovation. They presented him with a brick to be installed in the new meditation garden. Etched on it are the words he has used over and over during the last year, "We're getting there."

—April 6, 2001

Fred Bauer, Seventy-Fourth Grand Master of Freemasons

"It's a very humbling honor to be in this role. You're like the king and the president, all wrapped up in one," said Fred Bauer. On April 17, 1998, Fred received a phone call asking him to report to the Grand Lodge of Freemasons in Boston, a place he had visited often in his thirty-three years of being a Mason in the North Reading Lodge. His subsequent nomination and election to the third-highest position in the world's largest fraternal organization culminated in a grand ceremony of installation at the Tremont Street headquarters on December 27, 1998. There were 1,200 attendees.

Having served now seven months of his three-year term as the 74th Grand Master of Freemasons in Massachusetts, Fred is finding this honor to be an extraordinarily time-consuming endeavor. The grand master's calendar from June 2 to September 28 is printed on the inside back cover of *The Trowel*, listing forty-two events Fred has attended or will attend over the summer months. Most of them are in Massachusetts, but there are also the DeMolay International meeting in Kansas City, the Shrine Imperial Session in Dallas, Texas, and the Supreme Council of the Scottish Rite in Atlantic City, New Jersey. At this last event Fred will be invested with the Thirty-third Degree, the highest honor any Mason can receive.

"As grand master, I automatically became CEO of five corporations: Grand Lodge, Inc., Masonic Home, Inc., in Charleton, Samuel Crocker Lawrence Library, Grand Lodge Museum, Masonic Education and Charity Trust. I'm in the Grand Lodge in Boston usually three to five days a week, and out almost every evening and most weekends."

On a typical week this past July, Fred attended a rally of over 1,200 Masonic families who were camping at the Franklin County Fairgrounds; he led a strategic planning meeting in Boston, looking at the next five to ten years of the organization; and he visited with architects, reviewing renovation plans to assisted-living quarters at the Masonic home in Charleton, a 169-bed facility. "My calendar is chock-full," he said.

Why would a man who had just retired from a business career that spanned forty-five years of transportation management in Monsanto, Carling Brewing, Bird, Inc., and General Electric, devote this many hours to a volunteer position instead of playing golf? Part of the answer has to do with his commitment to service, part to connections with wonderful and committed people. Also fundamental to Fred's love of Masonry is family tradition; he is a fourth generation Mason.

The family story goes that on the day of his birth, April 21, 1936, Fred's maternal grandfather, Worshipful Alfred J. Kirby of Beacon Lodge No. 3, St. Louis, Missouri, signed a petition for his new grandson's start in fraternal life. "When he visited my mother and me for the first time, my grandfather actually came to our home with the petition and a check to cover the initiation. I was the first grandson; all of my previous cousins were girls." Fred joined DeMolay, a Masonic youth organization, when he was fourteen.

On Fred's first date with his wife, Kay Probst, he took her to a DeMolay dance at a Masonic hall in St. Louis. "Fred sat behind me in study hall," remembered Kay. "He asked to borrow my pencil one day. One thing led to another ... "

After earning a bachelor of science degree in business administration at Washington University in St. Louis, Fred took a job in 1956 with Monsanto Chemical Company in St. Louis. A promotion and transfer in 1965 found the young couple and two of their three daughters in North Reading, Massachusetts, looking for a house. Not surprisingly, all three daughters eventually joined North Reading Rainbow Assembly No. 103, serving in the highest leadership role there as worthy advisors.

In the early 1960s, Bigham Road was a new development off Route 62; Carl Bigham Sr., the developer, showed Fred number eight, just a frame. "We made an offer, and Kay flew up from St. Louis the next weekend for final approval. We thought we might stay two or three years," recalls Fred. He always assumed he would join the Masons in St. Louis when he returned there. Thirty-four years later, Bigham Road is still home.

Settled in North Reading, in 1968 Fred K. Bauer became a member of the North Reading Lodge, which at the time held its meetings in the Third Meeting House on the Common. Now housed at 283 Park Street, this local, "blue" lodge has over 200 members; one is his grandson, Keith Carl. Fred presides over the 279 lodges to which 53,000 Mason brothers belong, including four lodges in Panama, two in Japan, three in Chile, and one in Guantanamo Bay, Cuba. These international lodges grew to accommodate United States armed forces stationed in various locations during and following wars.

Founded in 1733 and being the oldest Grand Lodge in the United States, the Massachusetts Masons are very ceremonial. They are proud of the patriots and famous men they count as members. Paul Revere, like Fred, was a grand master of the Massachusetts Grand Lodge, as was Dr. Joseph Warren, the general who died at Bunker Hill, and Dr. Samuel Crocker Lawrence for whom the city to our north is named.

Masons have played a significant role in shaping life in the United States as we know it. Ralph Bellamy who wrote the Pledge of Allegiance was a Mason. Frederick A. Bartholdi, a Mason, designed the Statue of Liberty. Aviator Charles Lindberg was a Mason. Daniel Carter Beard, a Mason, organized the Boy Scouts of America. Dr. Alexander Fleming, a Mason, discovered penicillin. Roy Rogers, John Wayne and Gene Autry, America's favorite cowboy actors, were all Masons. Henry Ford, Walter Chrysler, Ransom Olds, all Masons, had a hand in creating the automobiles we drive. Even Kentucky Fried Chicken was started by a Mason, Harland Sanders.

Invited to become a grand master, Mason George Washington went off to run the country instead. Harry S. Truman, on the other hand, was grand master of the Missouri Masons the same year he served in the U. S. Senate. Fred loves the story about President Teddy Roosevelt, a Mason, who attended a meeting near his Long Island Estate where none other than his gardener was worshipful master. He likes this story because it illustrates an important tenet of Masonry. "Masons greet everyone 'on the level.' We recognize you as a person, not for what you have," explains Fred.

The tools Masons use in their trade are symbols for deeply held beliefs of Masons and emblematic of their three stages of membership. The first degree of membership uses the gavel to remind the Entered Apprentice of his dependence on others and his subordination to God. In the second degree, Fellowcraft, the square, level and plumb reinforce the central theme of brotherly love and service. The trowel represents the third degree, encouraging the Master Mason candidate to reflect on the end of life and on the value of faithfulness to his promise.

All of the symbolism and traditions date prior to the building of King Solomon's Temple in Israel. Depending on their level of competency, workers at the time were paid in corn, wine or oil, symbols then, and now, for health, plenty and peace. Artisans guarded, treasured and passed on their secrets of geometry and physics.

Fred emphasizes, "Masons is not a secret organization, but it is an organization with secrets. Most of our meetings are public." One must be twenty-one and male to become a member, but beyond that the Masons are open to men from all ethnicities and all religions. "All meetings begin and end with a prayer to the Supreme Architect of the Universe," he says. "For example, on the alter you might find the Bible, the Koran or the [Bhagavad-] Gita, whichever holy book is applicable to the membership."

Masons are very visible in their community service projects. The largest philanthropic organization in the world, United States, Masons give two million dollars to charity daily. Masons are the founders and sponsors of the Shriners Burn Hospitals and the Shriners Orthopedic Hospitals, both offering entirely free services to their patients.

Masons are the largest group of blood donors to the American Red Cross, giving 20,000 pints annually in Massachusetts. They run schizophrenia research programs, an eye foundation, a Masonic retirement home, and are the largest single supporter of Drug Abuse Resistance Education (DARE).

A special Massachusetts project, the Mason's Child Identification Program or CHIP, caught the public eye last February when the Masonic hall in Quincy had parents and children lined up to enroll. Grand Master Fred Bauer was on hand as News Center 5, News 4, Fox 25, Channel 56, News 7, and New England Cable News reported this innovative system that has been fingerprinting and videotaping Massachusetts children for almost three years. Serving the children has always been a focus for Fred. Taking the name of that maternal grandfather who first signed him up, Fred was Kirby the Clown with the Aleppo Shrine Temple Clown Unit for many years.

In his first letter to the readership of *The Trowel* this spring, Fred writes: "When you first became a Mason, you were asked, 'What came you here to do?' ... We [as Masons] continue a rich, proud heritage of men committed to self-improvement and helping others. We strive to show our pride through words and deeds. ... you and I have the opportunity— no, the responsibility—to make a real difference."

—August 20, 1999

Joan McLaughlin, Compassionate Friend for Bereaved Parents

On August 8, 1969, at 5:00 A.M., Joan McLaughlin, North Reading, mother of seventeen-month-old Gale, hung up the telephone and turned to her husband, "Somebody is playing a terrible trick on us." Mick dialed the hospital and a nurse confirmed that their daughter Gale, sick with a high fever for only one day, and admitted to the hospital the previous evening, had died in the night of the most virulent form of bacterial spinal meningitis.

"Luckily we were smart enough not to drive ourselves," remembered Joan. As the sky grew light, they sat, instead, on the front steps of their home on Meade Road waiting for Mick's parents, numb.

In those days parents were not permitted to stay overnight in the hospital with their children, hospitals sometimes delivered devastating information by telephone, and hospital personnel handed the mothers tranquilizers, expecting fathers to "be strong."

Six months after Gale died, Joan read in the North Reading paper that another mother, Ada Mongiello, had lost a three-year-old daughter, Ami, to cancer.

"At the time I thought, 'I'm really losing my mind here. If I could talk to one other parent who was going through the same thing . . .'" After writing a note of sympathy, Joan met Ada, and there began a friendship of mutual support. "We grieved together."

Eight years later, in 1976, when Joan saw in the paper that bereaved parents, Dorothy and John Chipman, had jformed a chapter of Compassionate Friends in Lynnfield, she was drawn to her first meeting.

The Compassionate Friends is a self-help organization that offers friendship and understanding to bereaved parents and siblings. Their purpose is to promote and aid parents in the positive resolution of the grief experienced upon the death of their child, and to foster the physical and emotional health of bereaved parents and siblings.

Madeleine Hill, in one monthly newsletter suggests, "Grief is a normal reaction, universally but uniquely experienced. Each person deals with death and all the losses associated with that death in a personal and individual way. ... With grief, there is an opportunity to grow, if we are able to take the risks. ... One must go through periods of numbness that are harder to bear than grief. Otherwise, scar tissue will seal off the wound and no growth will follow."

Founded in England in 1969 when a hospital chaplain brought two sets of grieving parents together to give each other support, Compassionate Friends is now a worldwide organization. A grieving couple in Florida founded the first chapter in the United States with the help of Reverend Simon Stephens, the British cleric. Chapters now exist in twenty-eight countries, with 600 active groups in the United States. The national office in Oak Brook, Illinois, coordinates resource catalogues, regional training for facilitators and an annual national convention.

This year's twenty-first national convention in Nashville, Tennessee, will feature Reg and Maggie Green, whose seven-year-old son, Nicholas, was killed in Italy by gunfire as he traveled with his family. Jan Howard, Grand Ole Opry singer who lost three of her four children will perform at the close of the weekend. Joan McLaughlin has attended two of these conventions and countless regional workshops. She has given workshops on sensitivity training to hospital personnel, funeral directors and teachers.

A year after her first meeting, Joan, along with North Reading residents Tom and Jean O'Hare, who lost their fifteen-year-old daughter, Jeannie, to leukemia, assumed leadership of the Northshore/Boston Chapter of Compassionate Friends. All three served in this role for thirteen years. That first year, the Aldersgate Methodist Church, 235 Park Street, extended its welcome. Ever since, more than twenty-five members have met there the first Monday of the month, 7:30 P.M., to offer hope and comfort to newly bereaved parents and to one another.

"I used to say to Jean and Tom, 'Wouldn't it be great if no one's child died this week, and no one new came through the door tonight?' But they come. They find us."

Every parent's grief is devastating, but suicide and murder are perhaps the toughest, Joan observes. Parents of murder victims are not only dealing with their grief, but also with the legal system and perhaps the press. Parents of children who have committed suicide deal with that nagging fear that they might have dissuaded their child, even though the death may not have been preventable. Says this month's bulletin, "Forgiveness is not a single act, but a lifestyle, and it is in forgiveness that we can find freedom from the ghosts and shadows of life."

Designed by a bereaved parent, John Fisher in 1975, the logo of Compassionate Friends shows two open hands in the foreground with the small figure of a child in the distance. At one meeting a grieving mother shared her living child's question, "Are those hands reaching out to get my sister back?"

"No," the mother replied. "I think they are letting go."

—*June 1, 1998*

Helen Eisenhaure, Quilter

The nice thing about winter is that you have an "excuse to stay inside and quilt," said Helen Eisenhaure. As I sat in her cozy living room, she unfolded her quilts one by one: The skating Santa with hearts rising from his crooked pipe, the spiky purple iris, the queen-sized Ohio Star quilt in black, aqua and magenta.

When Helen first moved to North Reading in 1958, she taught fifth and sixth grade at Batchelder School. After her marriage to Alfred Eisenhaure in 1960, she stayed home to raise her four children. Returning to the North Reading Public Schools eight years later as a regular substitute teacher, she held this position for fifteen years. More recently, Helen's association with the schools was in the SEEM program, working with developmentally delayed teens as their vocational coordinator. Always a teacher, in her retirement Helen continues to teach. For the past twenty years she has taught quilting to beginning and advanced classes in Reading and North Reading.

"In the beginner class I teach a sampler or wall-hanging so students can experiment with a variety of skills: appliqué, piecing, how to make an eight-pointed star, hand and machine quilting." As the weeks go along, Helen also demonstrates more advanced techniques like stained glass, where the quilter applies handmade bias tape between the squares, or bargello, a geometric design that runs vertically. "The girls in the classes develop new friends. Many remain friends for years," said Helen.

When did Helen's interest in quilting begin? "My grandmother, Carolyn Hersey, used to spend winters with us in Concord, New

Hampshire, where my father had a dairy farm. Grandmother quilted, but I didn't pay much attention." Youngest of twelve children, Helen marveled that her mother, Mehitable Bean, had time to sew at all. "Farmers wives exchanged grain sacks. Chicken and cow feed came in printed cotton bags." Helen's grandmother would piece utility bed quilts during those long winter months. The women wasted nothing.

In 1976 Helen took a North Reading adult education course in quilting with Lucy LeGrow. Other students in that class were Gerry Messinger, Effie Gaw, Madeline Thomson, Leone Correlle, Jean Richards, Edna Ferrell, Barbara King, and Shirley Loveys. Some of these women are still active in the North Parish Quilters, a regional group of 150 who meet monthly at the Union Congregational Church in North Reading.

"Lucy was a wonderful teacher," remembered Helen. "She really inspired us to quilt. Friendly and patient, she was a very creative woman." Lucy coordinated the making of a quilt to commemorate the 1976 bicentennial celebration. Many of her students worked on this treasure depicting the Putnam House, Turner Farm, Flint Library, the Third Meeting House, and other historic North Reading buildings.

In 1977 Lucy retired to Florida where she continued to quilt, and to teach quilting, until she passed away a few years ago. It was after Lucy moved away that Helen began teaching the quilting classes in North Reading's adult education.

Nancy Simonds took her first quilting lessons from Helen Eisenhaure. "I made the ugliest quilt in the world," she said. "My first attempt had too many colors. I didn't even write my name on it! Margi Rasche and Judy Haynes made really pretty samplers." A nurse at Melrose-Wakefield Hospital recovery room, Nancy has made baby quilts and full bed quilts for each of her seven grandchildren and for each of her three children. "I only make them for people I love," she said. A king-sized quilt can take six months to a year to complete.

One of seven students in Helen's first quilting class, Brenda Lane now teaches courses herself, both at North Reading adult education and at Mary Rose's Quilts and Treasures in Reading. "Helen is an inspiration to all of us," said Brenda. "Quilting brings people together; it's a young art."

Laurie Thies opened Mary Rose's Quilts and Treasures in April 1998. Named for her two grandmothers, first-generation Italians who made not only quilts, but lace, sweaters, and wedding dresses, Mary Rose's flier describes twenty-one different classes in quilting this winter. Stocked with fabric, rulers, and "fat quarter" bins filled with scraps of cotton, the store caters to the needs of the beginner and more advanced quilter.

Department manager for fabric and crafts at the new Wal-Mart in North Reading, Terry McGonagle is a serious quilter and also a loyal member of the North Parish Quilters. "I take so much pleasure in creating with fabric," said Terry. Even though she works a forty-hour week in the Wal-Mart fabric department, Terry finds time to sew almost every day. "I have seven sewing machines and subscribe to five different quilting magazines."

Terry enjoys quilting workshops when she can get away. Once a year in November she goes to the juried show at the Westford, Massachusetts, Regency Hotel. Occurring annually for four days in July, the Vermont Quilt Fest is another popular regional quilting event she has attended.

"One March," recalled Terry, "I went to a quilting week-end at the 4-H Center in Ashland. You take your own sewing machine, and they give you a place to sleep and to sew until you drop. You don't even have to change out of your bathrobe. It was great!" said Terry.

Like Terry, Helen has enjoyed the Vermont Quilt Fest and other quilting events. "We think we quilt in New England," mused Helen, "but you should go to Lancaster, Pennsylvania, or Paducah, Kentucky." Paducah holds a quilting conference and juried show every April. Some of the country's leading quilters give workshops there, which Helen has attended.

The North Parish Quilters sponsor their own yearly show in March. Over one hundred quilts made by members of the group hang in the Union Congregational Church Parish Hall in March. Members sell boutique and quilted items, and Mary Rose's shop has fabric and supplies on hand.

The North Parish Quilters meet on the second Wednesday of each month. With a membership of 150, there is a waiting list to join this popular group that began in Lucy's living room. Their monthly newsletter, *Quarter Inch Press,* keeps the membership updated on the block of the month, quarter raffle themes, and mystery quilt progress. As an outreach, members regularly make small quilts for newborn preemies, and angel quilts for stillborns at Mass General Hospital.

"Last month each member brought in blue fabric blocks for the newborn quilts," said Kathy Rinaldi. "I bought some teddy bear and cloud-print flannel sashing, finished the quilts, and took them to the hospital. It's good to be able to help in a small way."

Last month's meeting of the North Parish Quilters featured a trunk show, a lecture/demonstration by The Keepsake Quilters of New Hampshire. At another meeting this fall, Cranston Printworks of Webster, Massachusetts, presented information about the design and fabrication of cotton for quilts.

What's next? Millennium quilts! Helen Eisenhaure has already cut 600 two-inch squares of the 2,000 squares that will make a bed quilt to mark the year 2000. "There are many types of millennium patterns. The Internet has exchanges, how-to's, mystery quilt projects, quilting information." Not yet adept with this technology, Helen relies on her granddaughter, Brianna, to find the Internet information for her.

Helen is so enthusiastic about quilting that her greatest challenge is to finish one project before jumping into the next. Currently she is stitching a lighthouse on a snow-covered island, with wreathes in each window and the deep blue sea below. "The greatest pleasure I get in quilting is working with the colors and seeing the design evolve. In a beginner class of twelve, the same project has twelve different results because of fabric color and personal choice," said Helen.

—January 29, 1999

Margaret "Peggy" Parker Turns Ninety

"I'm glad there are only two candles," Margaret "Peggy" Parker announced at her Putnam House birthday party on May 3 as more than ninety well-wishers gathered to honor her in the building she helped to save. The two candles were a nine and a zero. On this occasion of party sandwiches, pineapple punch, and tea in flowered china cups, Peggy received not only a engraved silver Paul Revere bowl from the North Reading Historical Society, which she helped found some fifty years ago, but also proclamations from the North Reading Selectmen, House of Representative Speaker Thomas Finneran and the Massachusetts governor himself,

Paul Celluci, congratulating her for her many year's service to the town, especially with respect to things historic.

Peggy and her husband, Bob, moved to North Reading in 1940 yearning for a country home with some land. At that time their section of Haverhill Street, lined with fourteen sugar maples, had four houses on it. Bob was a civil engineer in Boston, building bridges and designing dams, but in his off hours he and his new bride were farmers on their several acres at Long Hill Farm. First, they set out Baldwin, Cortland and Northern Spy apple trees in the side yard, and next there were the bees.

One day while Bob was in Boston, Peggy got a call from the Andover railroad station to come immediately to pick up her Railway Express shipment of bees. Bees other than the ones ordered were swarming the hive, attracted by the queen. Peggy immediately got in her 1936 Ford convertible, the same one Gig Stephens now drives in the Memorial Day Parade, and sped north to claim the bees from a distraught Andover railroad station master.

Next, Bob and Peggy bought a heifer from Old Mr. Putnam. "Old Put" himself delivered the calf, riding in the front seat of Reuben Eisenhaure's milk truck, the heifer, which was the size of a great Dane, on his lap. There were three cows in all (later additions being a Jersey named "Silver" and a Guernsey named "Star") whose milk the Parkers shared with their neighbors during the war years.

"Both of us came from old Yankee families where you made do; you didn't borrow, you paid your own way and helped out where you could. We were brought up never to complain about our own life, but to be ready to help anyone in need ... "

In the late 1950s that philosophy led Peggy to the county commissioners meeting in Cambridge with pictures in hand of the fourteen magnificent sugar maples, marked for removal so that the county could widen Haverhill Street. Telling her friends she would chain herself to the trees if necessary to prevent their demise, she was relieved that her appearance at the hearing was enough to save the maples.

With equal zeal in the early 1960s, Peggy helped to save the Putnam House. At that time the property was for sale, and there were rumors of various commercial ventures including plans for a supermarket and a strip mall on the Putnam House site. Historical society members were frantic! Peggy, along with Elizabeth Batchelder,

Lillian Butler and others, went door to door collecting signatures to petition Town Meeting to purchase the home of the first pastor in North Parish, Reverend Putnam. Their efforts were rewarded.

The Historical Society, formed by ladies from the Upland Club in 1952 and incorporated in 1961 with the help of Lawyer Charles Statuti, now had a home. So it probably should not have surprised the town when two years ago at age eighty-eight, Peggy stood up at Town Meeting to exhort North Reading to preserve Damon Tavern (the former town library building) with its priceless Rufus Porter murals.

"I did. I got quite irate. One of the selectmen wanted to sell it to a private buyer and I couldn't take it! And I begged them, 'Don't sell it, not tonight.' "

Founder, curator, president, secretary and custodian of the Historical Society over many years, Peggy has also served the town as library trustee, Hilltop Nursery schoolteacher, Congregational Church historian and grand marshal of the Memorial Day parade. Peggy well deserves special recognition on her ninetieth birthday.

"I really do love North Reading. A very special place, it's inevitable it had to change. But life doesn't stand still. The number of people at my party on Sunday amazed me. I don't have any relatives left; it's hard being near the end of a family line. People have been so kind."

—*May 11, 1998*

Nelda Rouillard, Artist and Author

It is ten years since North Reading artist Nelda Rouillard published her children's book *Papa's Red Britches,* committing to paper the legend that tells how John Upton acquired his land from the Sachem Indian Wenepoykin.

The story goes this way: John and Eleanor Upton were out for a ride on their horses one Sunday in the 1600s and came to the meadows, woods and river we now call North Reading. They met the Native-American Wenepoykin who, taking a fancy to Upton's attire, offered to exchange his land for the red riding pants John Upton was wearing. Upton gave him the britches for the land and rode back home wearing his wife Eleanor's petticoat.

It is a story Nelda first read in 1976 during this country's bicentennial. Wanting to share this amusing legend with her grandchildren, Nelda painted ten watercolors to illustrate Upton's purchase. Then she wrote the story with a few embellishments of her own. She dreamed of publishing it, but had little time to pursue that dream until 1982 when she retired from sixteen years of preschool teaching at the First Baptist Day School in Reading.

It was at a gathering hosted by the North Reading Arts Council in the late 1980s that Nelda met Carol Lundgren, the second director of Arts Workshop for Children. "Nelda was pretty discouraged about the book," said Carol. "She had written letters to some publishers, but was resigned there would be only one copy of *Papa's Red Britches* for her grandchildren to fight over."

Charmed by the story, Carol saw the possibility of the legend becoming a play that students in Arts Workshop might present. "Because I had just worked with Nancy Parsons and Dick Amsterdam on the production and marketing of Reverend Hal Fohlin's book, *Life is for Living,* I felt I could help Nelda," said Carol. And, help she did.

Managing the actual production of the book, Nancy and Dick agreed to donate their time, expertise and connections. Nelda insisted the book be hardbound with color illustrations, a real keepsake edition. Because this was an expensive proposition, fund-raising needed to take on a community spirit. The Flint Library Bookworms, led by Colleen Dolan, hosted a Petticoats and Red Britches costume ball to pay for the color separation process of the ten watercolor illustrations, and Nelda came to the dance dressed as Eleanor Upton, carrying five dolls she made to represent the characters in the book. Later Nelda would visit numerous Reading and North Reading elementary classrooms in Eleanor's garb, reading *Papa's Red Britches* and encouraging young people to never give up on their dreams, because look what happened to her when everyone helped with the project!

In another fund-raiser for the book, the North Parish Quilters under Helen Eisenhaure's direction, created a quilt reflecting colonial and Native American motifs, and sold raffle tickets raising $1,000 for the book's expenses. Cindy Harvey of Reading was the winner.

A mere month after publication all 750 numbered and signed copies of *Papa's Red Britches* had been sold. At the book-warming, grandson Ryan, remarked, "I can't believe it was dedicated to me (and the other grandchildren), not many people have books dedicated to them." After the North Reading Arts Council granted money to frame the original art work, Nelda donated it to the Flint Library children's room; she also gave the library's new children's room all the proceeds from her book, which amounted to $3,000.

That fall, Arts Workshop for Children offered a theater class based on *Papa's Red Britches,* which Nancy Stewart and Jayne Reilly taught. Narrated by Nelda that December, the play featured fifteen North Reading youth as Uptons, Indians, and woodland creatures.

"We invited the small children in the audience to come forward to sit near the stage," remembers Carol. "We had chins on the stage; they were drinking it in."

Upton descendants from Wakefield, Massachusetts, to Tubac, Arizona, came to the book-warming party on November 19, 1989, in the Building on the Common. Seventh- and eighth-generation descendants of John Upton, a farmer who arrived in Salem, Massachusetts, from Scotland in 1651, and subsequently fathered thirteen children, began to correspond with one another.

Harriet Given, seventh generation, wrote to Carol, "My family and I wish to thank you for arranging the book warming, the visits to our ancestral home (on Upton Avenue) and to the Putnam House ... It was exciting to see again the George F. Root organ which stood in the front parlor of the Upton homestead when I was a child. I recall playing it and, on two occasions, hearing the wedding march for the marriages of Louise Upton Mack and Carrie Upton Thomas. ... At the book warming Nelda looked so attractive in her beautiful costume as she graciously autographed hundreds of books."

Barbara O'Brien, who is writing a history of the town of North Reading, remembers hearing the Upton legend when she was in grade school here in town. Having researched the deeds for many properties in North Reading, Barbara explains that the town of Reading got this land in 1651. By 1658, lots had been laid out in a diagonal configuration north of Ten Rod Way, the first road through North Reading, which follows along the Ipswich River.

Because he was a farmer, John Upton was interested in the entire prime farming real estate he could buy on the north side of Ten Rod Way, now Elm Street or Route 62, as well as the Upton Avenue land behind Moynihan Lumber. "All of the deeds for John Upton from the late 1600s are recorded at the Registry of Deeds," says Barbara.

Were red trousers exchanged with Native Americans? Not likely. "But it is probably the most popular town legend, and one of my favorites. Isn't it a good story?" says Barbara.

In her colorful version of the legend, "Nelda's illustrations recall a plain and schematic drawing that both colonists and Native Americans would commit to their diaries and journals," observes Don Doyle, another local artist. "Curators refer to them as ledger-book drawings. Into these pen-line illustrations Nelda pours a luminous and educated sense of color."

Nelda has been painting North Reading scenery for most of the forty-six years she has lived in the town. Having no art instruction in the one-room school house in Ephrata, Pennsylvania, where she grew up, Nelda took the business course in high school, and worked in a wholesale egg warehouse for twelve dollars a week when she graduated. She met her husband, Eddie, with whom she will celebrate fifty years of marriage this July, at a Hamilton Watch Company Christmas Dance in Lancaster, Pennsylvania. Eddie was in the army at the time and stationed near her home.

"We corresponded for a time and then became engaged. I raised a few eyebrows when I moved to the Malden YMCA to be near him." On the GI Bill, Eddie attended the Fenway Optical School, launching his forty-five-year career as an optician.

When they were first married, it was Eddie who encouraged Nelda to take her first painting class with a Mr. Coletta in Arlington. Eddie is still encouraging and praising his wife's artistic accomplishments. Their home is filled with art: water colors of a Marblehead cove and the Boston swan boats, Currier and Ives stenciling on the dining room chairs, yard sale tray tables transformed with Tasha Tudor-style trillium and columbine.

Nelda's best-known image, her motif No. 1, is the North Reading Common in winter and summer. She has painted this design on more than forty barrel staves and many canvases. Recently commissioned to paint the Hillview Country Club, she also produced a fare watercolor of Batchelder School for retiring principal Neal Sanders.

Nelda has thought about writing stories for her grandchildren about her days in the one-room school in Pennsylvania Dutch Country. Would she illustrate it? "I think I wrote *Papa's Red Britches* so I could illustrate it. I couldn't be happy without illustration," she said.

—*May 10, 1999*

Little School Ribbon Cutting

On Sunday, October 25, Principal William P. Leccese will welcome students, teachers and town dignitaries at 2:30 P.M. to cut the ribbon that officially reopens the renovated E. Ethel Little Elementary School.

Standing before the color guard made up of fourth-grade Cub Scouts and Girl Scouts, fifth-grader Ashley Forgione will say the Pledge of Allegiance. Peter Allen, Little School music teacher, has written "Hymn for Recorder," which the Little School Recorder Ensemble will perform; Little School Chorus will sing "Seasons Change." Both musical groups have been rehearsing this fall in their cathedral ceilinged music room in the new wing, a decided improvement from the cafeteria stage where Peter Allen previously taught.

Built in 1958, the Little School was named to honor E. Ethel Little, a graduate of North Reading Public Schools herself. Born in 1882, Ethel lived at the corner of Park and Main where Cota Funeral Home now stands, until her death in 1960. Graduated from Salem Normal School, now Salem State Teacher's College, Ethel served on the North Reading school committee for twenty-one years. Fran Mague remembers the elementary school's namesake well since her father, Daniel Shay, for whom the high school auditorium is named, served with Ethel during the same twenty years.

"Mrs. Little used to recite the Gettysburg Address every Memorial Day. She was such an active woman; her sister, who also lived on Park Street, was so very proud of Ethel. 'Sister could do anything,' she would say."

In addition to serving on the school committee, Ethel was also clerk of the First Baptist Church for many years, a member of the Upland Club, Daughters of the American Revolution, and North Reading Grange. She wrote North Reading copy for the *Reading Chronicle* and composed poetry for special occasions. President Truman awarded her a silver scroll for her many years of service to the Red Cross.

Fran Mague remembers that Ethel's house on Park Street at one time housed a branch of the North Reading Library for the convenience of patrons on the west side of town. Certainly she will be present in spirit at the ribbon cutting on Sunday.

The three-and-a-half-million dollar renovation, sixty-five percent of which is state reimbursed, is not the first change to the school. In 1969 there was a major addition. In 1990 the school closed due to declining enrollment; Principal Bill Leccese reopened the school in 1995 to serve preschool through grade three.

Today, Bill is beaming as he shows us the new 12,000 volume library, two new kindergarten rooms, three resource rooms, the twenty-five station computer lab, the soundproof music practice room, the art room with shiny kiln (purchased by the PTO).

"Before we opened the new wing it was pretty much 'art on a cart' or maybe 'art à la carte.' The new courtyard will have a butterfly garden." Bill points out. Katie Monahan, who co-chairs the PTO with Paula Bones, was thrilled when Eric's Greenhouse donated mums, pumpkins, a birdbath and bench last week to begin that beautification.

"The community is really pulling together, and it's a great feeling," says Katie.

—*June 23, 1998*

Fran Mague, Daniel Shay, Rufus Potter and the Flints

From the late 1930s to the early 1950s there was still only one school in North Reading, the Batchelder School, and only three residents served on the board of education: Arthur Conron, Ethel Little and Daniel Shay. Each time the school bell rings today, North Reading High School students pass the picture of Daniel Shay in the foyer of the auditorium named in his honor. Born into a family committed to education, Daniel's granddaughter, Ellen Mague, continues to work as a teacher's aide at the Hood School. Daniel's daughter, Fran Mague, still lives on Park Street in the same house Daniel bought in 1929 when Fran was nine years old.

As we enter Fran's home, a white colonial built by George Flint for his son, George, in the early 1700s, we are immediately drawn to the umber-toned Rufus Porter murals extending down the hall, and the muted tree snaking up the staircase. The wide planks of the floor below were all taken up, refinished and refitted by Daniel Shay himself. Framed and hanging in the parlor, whose walls are also covered by Porter murals quite similar to those in the Damon Tavern ballroom, is a scroll from the Trade School Directors of Massachusetts, presented to Daniel at his retirement in 1950.

Beginning in 1911, Daniel taught carpentry and woodworking in a technical high school in Springfield. At the end of World War I, his employment brought him and his bride, Frances Ray, to Boston to begin work for the Massachusetts department of education. A champion of vocational education his entire life, Daniel is praised in the scroll for "rare wisdom, understanding and inspiration," and the "spirit of his principles," which he passed on to other educators as a teacher and, later as the Massachusetts state supervisor of industrial education.

Daniel first ran for North Reading School Committee in 1936 or 1937 when Fran was in high school. After losing his first election, subsequent elections led to twenty-two years of service on the committee. Since Batchelder School at that time educated students from first to ninth grade only, Fran was attending high school in Reading when her father was elected. By the time Daniel retired from the school committee, she was married to Charles Mague, also a teacher for the North Reading school system for many years.

Charles began teaching at the Batchelder School in 1951. "When the PTA had a party for the new teachers, my mother and father attended. They thought it was good politics to know the new teachers," said Fran. Having studied home economics and retail at Simmons College, Fran was working at the time in Boston for R. H. Stearns, the department store. She lived with her parents in the George Flint house.

"My mother returned from that party and said there were two new teachers. One was very good looking, she said. That was Dick York, the new physical education teacher. The other she said was not quite so good looking, but appeared to be a very nice man. His name was Charles Mague, the man who would become my husband."

Because he still lived in Littleton with his parents, Charles rented a room, as did many of the single faculty, at the Eaton Inn, which still stands next to the auto body store on Haverhill Street. The inn's owner, Hovey Eaton, was the janitor at Batchelder School; his wife, Ruby, ran the boarding house. "Ruby was a wonderful cook. She made delicious pecan rolls," remembered Fran.

Fran belonged to a dramatic group at St. Agnes Church on Woburn Street in Reading. Her mother's friend, Marea Murphy, who taught first grade at the Batchelder School and for whom the Murphy School was later named, mentioned that Charlie Mague had some dramatic talents, but no car.

"At St. Agnes, we were putting on the play, *Mr. Belvidere*. Some might remember Clifton Webb, the thin British-looking actor, and Robert Young starred in the popular movie version, *Sitting Pretty*. The local play had been cast, but the Korean War took a turn for the worse, and the two male leads had to leave because of the war," said Fran. One was called back to the Charlestown Navy yard; the other owned Kitty Snicker Cat Food, and, because of the war shortage of tin, he had to give full attention to his business that was in jeopardy.

Charlie, getting a ride to the audition in Fran's 1935 Plymouth with the rumble seat, tried out for both parts and landed the part Clifton Webb later played in the movie.

"When the play was over, Chuck asked me to go with him to the cast party. He needed a ride there, too," she said with a laugh. A romance evolved, which led to forty-three-and-a-half years of marriage.

At Batchelder School Charles taught math and English to Barbara O'Brien, Herbie Batchelder, Ned Larkin and Harry Hobbie, among others, who still live in North Reading. But after Fran and Charlie were married in 1952, they moved to Brockton where Charlie taught until 1966. By this time Fran's mother had passed away, and her father, Daniel, had retired from the North Reading School Committee, the auditorium having been named after him in 1958. "They wanted to name the new high school after my father, but he thought the name of the town should be on it. Naming the auditorium after him was a compromise," said Fran.

The George Flint Jr., House on Park Street stood vacant from 1963 to 1966, vandals throwing rocks through the windows, the weeds taking over the gardens.

In September 1966, the Magues moved back into Fran's childhood home, dusting off the sign the Daughters of the American Revolution (DAR) had nailed by the front door in the 1930s that read: "Built in 1713 by Sergeant George Flint for his son, George, who hither brought the fair Jerusha Pope for his bride. From this house many worthy descendants came, including Lt. John Flint who, with musket on shoulder, left to join the farmers and patriots at Concord and Lexington." Fran is convinced the date on the sign is not correct. She believes her home was more likely built by the Damon brothers in the mid- to late-1700s.

Since Jerusha Pope was related to the Popes of Salem, a shipping family like the Darbys and the Pickerings, Marea Murphy suggested Fran explore the Flint history at the Essex Institute in Salem, Massachusetts. When Fran went to the institute, a little bird of a woman pulled out dusty books confirming that young George indeed had wed a well-to-do bride in Jerusha.

George Flint's grandfather, Thomas, was the first Flint to cross the Atlantic. Fran's research at the Essex Institute showed that Thomas Flint bought land in Danvers from a Mr. Pickering for whom Pickering Wharf is named.

Giles Corey, convicted of being a warlock and pressed to death, witnessed and signed the deed to that Danvers transaction. Henry Wadsworth Longfellow later wrote a poem about Giles's tragic death.

The "mighty Ipswich River" lured Thomas Flint's son George to North Reading, according to Fran. Much wider and faster flowing in the 1700s than today, the river was an important source of power for the mills the Flints and others built.

George Flint built the home on Park Street for his son on the west side of town so that George Jr. could run the grist and sawmills the family owned. Trees felled from the west side of town were processed at the Flint sawmill near what is now Mill Street. The Flint family owned land on both sides of Park Street, the property extending all the way to the railroad tracks near Café Amore. The property remained in the Flint family until the late 1800s when the last Flint, owner of a coal and wood business in Charlestown, and not a very sound business man according to Fran, sold off parcels of the land to pay his debts.

"The painting of landscape murals depicting rural, sea coast and small town scenes flourished in New England between 1825 and 1840," explains a pamphlet from the Maine State Museum in Augusta. "Using water-based paints, the murals were applied to dry plaster walls, unlike frescoes where pigments are painted on wet plaster. In Maine alone, seventy examples of landscape murals in forty towns have been identified. Rufus Porter (1792–1884) is one of the best know regional mural painters. An extraordinary jack-of-all-trades, he was variously a teacher, writer, inventor, publisher and painter." Two of the four buildings he is known to have decorated in North Reading still stand.

Rufus Porter decorated the Damon Tavern ballroom walls in the early 1830s. The murals were discovered by members of the Historical Society in the late 1950s and, with the help of artist Barbara Blanchard, members of the society carefully removed the wallpaper covering them. Since its close in 1991 when the library it contained moved across the street, structural repairs to the Damon Tavern building have been extensive.

In the other local building with original Rufus Porter wall murals, the George Flint home, the artwork also was hidden under many layers of wallpaper for years and years. In the 1920s the Barber family, from whom the Shays purchased the property in 1929, removed the seven layers of wallpaper in the living room, and discovered islands, a lighthouse, trees and a sailing ship in scenes that looked very much like Newburyport. As he had for the Damon Tavern, Rufus Porter very likely stayed in the Flint house while he worked on the wall paintings.

"Peggy Parker got this house registered as a state historic property so that it would be saved," said Fran. Unlike the Van Heusen house on Main Street, which also had Rufus Porter murals and was torn down in the early 1960s, George Flint's home, with its Rufus Porter artwork, will be preserved.

The classification has already done some good. When the town repaired Park Street in the early 1980s, all the land for the widening came from the other side of the street. "I guess it did help," said Fran.

—November 12, 1999

Six
Something You Can't Learn

The Reverend Daniel Putnam House, 1720

Joe Gallagher, Hornet's Nest Sub Shop

"It has been twenty-six and a half years, and people told me I wouldn't last six months," said Joe Gallagher, proprietor of the Hornet's Nest sub shop on Park Street in North Reading.

Joe opened The Hornet's Nest on September 23, 1972. For ten years he had been working for General Electric in Wilmington as an instrument manufacturing supervisor. "I had worked my way up. I had forty-five people working for me, and I was ready for the funny farm. I had had enough."

He grew up in Lynn and attended St. Mary's High School with North Reading High School baseball coaches Frank Carey and Billy Deven. Red Sox baseball great Tony Conigliaro was also in their class. Everyone in Joe's family worked for G. E. According to Joe, everyone in Lynn worked for G. E.

Because his dad was in the service, and his mother was a full-time G. E. employee, it was Joe's Grandmother Bejtlich who really raised him and his sister, Nancy. "My Polish grandparents were from the old country. We had a little farm on the Saugus River with chickens, vegetables, a fruit orchard, flowers and a farm stand. Every morning before breakfast, I got eggs from the chicken coop for my grandmother."

Because Grandfather Gallagher died when Joe was only a year old, Joe never knew him, but he knew he was in the food business and owned Gallagher's Restaurant on Western Avenue across from the G. E. As a boy, Joe washed dishes next door at Red Glowick's restaurant while he attended a Polish grade school at St. Michael's.

In 1966, Joe and his new bride left Lynn to move to Peter Road, North Reading, nearer to his General Electric job in Wilmington. An avid skier through high school, Joe, at the time was renting a ski lodge with nine friends. "And guess who was the cook? I always loved to cook." As he considered leaving G. E. and thought about opening his own business, Joe liked the idea of working in the food industry.

In 1971 the grocery store scanner had not yet been invented, and there was only one fast-food store in North Reading, Mario's. Elmer Jones was closing his hardware store and selling his building; Joe Price was moving from Elmer's building to larger quarters in the new shopping strip on Elm Street, a few hundred yards away. Joe Gallagher approached Arthur Rodham, the new owner of the Jones building, and became his first tenant. Using the counter Joe Price left behind, Joe Gallagher began getting his space ready to open The Hornet's Nest.

Bill Cahill was working for Joe Regan at the time in a sub shop in Peabody. He remembers the day Joe Gallagher came into that shop asking his boss for advice about running a successful business. Joe Regan not only shared his expertise, he offered to loan Billy to help Joe Gallagher open up.

Billy Cahill really knew the sub shop business," said Joe Gallagher. "He trained me. He trained the kids. Without him I would have made too many mistakes. He was tough. Even though I owned the place, he'd set me straight. He was the master of subs," said Joe. Billy came to work with Joe on the Monday before the Hornet's Nest opened; he stayed three years.

"If you intend to do business you have to have equipment, inventory," said Billy. "Joe didn't really have too much." Having first a two-foot grill, within a few days he had purchased a four-foot grill and additional freezers. With lines out the door and around the corner on opening day, Joe said, " I didn't figure it would go off that well. In two days I had sold all my tonic."

Billy was a great asset. "You could throw thirty subs at him, and he'd remember them all," said Joe.

"Joe picked up the business quick," said Billy. It had to be an advantage being close to the high school. The hornet is the school's mascot, hence the shop's name. In the early seventies the high school had an open campus; kids could leave school and get a sub during the day. Wednesday early release days were, and still are, a very busy time.

The first student employee at The Hornet's Nest was Colin Bonfanti. His grandfather owned Bonfanti's Restaurant on Main Street where Ristorante Daniela is now, but Joe did not know that until later. "I was doing carpentry work in the shop before we opened, and I'd see this kid walk by on his way home from school. One day I called out the door to him, 'Hey, I want to talk with you. Would you like a job?' Colin was with me six or seven years!"

It takes a certain type of young person to adapt to the speed, pressure and focus of working in a place like The Hornet's Nest. "Kids who make it past the training tend to stay," explained John Mastro, a six-year veteran of the shop. Dave Oliva, who is still putting himself through college on cheese steak money like John Mastro did before him, remembers the fast pace of the first weeks, and wanting to quit. "Joe says, 'If you can work here, you can work anywhere.' He expects a lot of you. I never thought I'd do what Johnny Mastro could: a dozen subs behind him. Sometimes it gets so busy you have to take the phone off the hook," said Dave.

North Reading Police Detective Tom Romeo worked for Joe Gallagher from 1979 to 1982. "Joe wouldn't allow for mistakes. He'd know if there was a crumb on the floor. There were employees we knew weren't going to make it, but I loved the job. Joe was the greatest; I invited him to my wedding!"

Joe usually keeps new hires on for at least six months. "If things don't improve you have a talk," said Joe. "Maybe they'd be better suited to work some place else." Joe could program the register to tell his employee the change, but he wants his help to think. "We give them little tests: how to take a phone order, for example. Everything is abbreviations. We all have to be in the same lane when it gets busy."

In the slow times, according to John, Joe's motto is "If you have time to lean, you have time to clean." Ricky Howe, Chris Beale, Laurie Fowler, Joe's three sons, his two nephews, and now Nate Chesley and Adam DiGiovanni are just a few of the many young people who have survived Joe's training. His family has also worked for him over the years, especially making the meatballs in the early years: his father, sister, Nancy, and his wife, Linda.

"My wife is behind me one hundred percent. She often covers for me. We are a team."

Who is The Hornet Nest's best customer? Would it be Red Sox pitcher Bob Stanley who used to live in town, or the Bruins's Dave Christian? Celtics's coach Chris Ford or Jim Luscutoff? The signed pictures of these former super stars hang on the paneled wall next to a map of the ski trails at Sunday River. All of these sports figures have eaten subs at The Hornet's Nest. But Joe thinks his best customer is the regular who orders the same thing, which apparently most of us do.

David Oliva may not have known my name, but he knew that my husband orders a cheese steak with tomatoes every Saturday at about one o'clock.

John Mastro recalls, "I met a friend of my brother-in-law at a family gathering—'large steak bomb, no peppers,' I said after shaking his hand. 'How'd you know that?' he said."

Joe's very best customer is a man who goes to the bank every Thursday to cash his check. Joe doesn't know his name. They seldom speak. "He always orders a Pepsi, bag of chips, cheese and egg. When I see his truck I start cracking the eggs. The man even called once when he was going on vacation. Didn't want me to start making his sandwich if I saw a truck like his," Joe said.

Worst customer? There are three kinds. The first is the one who stares at the menu for five minutes with a line out the door, and then wants to order an item that is not on the list. Or insists on a toasted roll. "We don't toast," says Joe. "Don't you have an oven out back?" they want to know. "It's a really special customer who wants you to make something you don't have."

Another problematic customer is the one that changes his or her mind when the sub is just about ready. But the most annoying customer for Joe is the one who gives the new employee a hard time. "I defend the kid," said Joe. "Everybody's got to start somewhere. Difficult customers are not usually the local regulars. If you come in a lot you know everybody is working hard here."

Besides working hard, what is the secret to his success? Consistency of the product, Joe feels, is at the core.

"I buy only the best beef; I trim it myself. Vendors want to sell you substitutes. A cheaper mayonnaise, for example. But mayo is a big factor in the taste of your tuna salad or your seafood salad. I don't want any substitutes. Keep the quality up and the prices down. The same customers will keep coming," he said.

What's next? "If I still worked for G. E., I'd have thirty-six years service and five weeks vacation now," he said. The hardest part of being self-employed is having no vacation unless you close the store. However, the advantages far outweigh the disadvantages. Because Joe owned his own business all these years, he was able to make time as his sons were growing up to coach their baseball teams. "Lots of guys travel for a living; it is a real privilege today to spend time with your kids." Now that his boys are grown (Ask him about his twin grandsons!), Joe has more recently coached the downhill ski team at St. John's Prep School. The best part of being self-employed is that "I only have to answer to me."

Joe and his wife talk about heading north someday, maybe opening a shop in North Conway. They both love to ski, actually having met skiing on Black Mountain. When the building changed hands this year, Joe thought it might be his year to move on. Lucky for North Reading, he signed another five-year lease.

"What keeps me in this place is the people. Especially when they come back and tell me, 'I've been out of town for twenty years, and I can't believe the cheese steak is as good as it was twenty years ago.' "

—*June 1, 1999*

Lou Greenstein, Culinary Collector

If you had two hundred cranberry grinders and twenty-five rolling pins, would it change the way you fixed Thanksgiving dinner?

Author of three books relating to culinary history, North Reading resident Lou Greenstein of Epicurean Consulting is a collector of cooking objects and kitchen memorabilia. The lower level of his home on Sunset Avenue houses 15,000 kitchen gadgets, 6,000 cookbooks and 4,000 or 5,000 menus; he has lost count.

On a short tour of the lower level of the split-entry home he shares with his wife, Zelma, son, Joshua, and daughter, Rachel, we first stand before a large cabinet at the foot of the stairs. The top shelf holds all manner of butter molds and butter prints; the second tier has candy-making equipment. On the third shelf are perhaps 150 can and bottle openers, some dating back to before 1900. The next shelf is home to corkscrews, ice picks and nutcrackers, even a squirrel-shaped one. Lou removes a fifteen-inch, tin-lined bunny mold once used to make large chocolate Easter confections at the Schrafft's Candy factory in Somerville. "Schrafft's even had a repair shop to retin such molds," he explains.

As we enter the first room of this tour, Lou directs our attention to the walls; a photograph of his grandmother's candy store in Philadelphia seventy-five years ago, an antique cast-iron commercial cake pan with six rounds, and a framed Jell-O ad by artist Maxfield Parrish are some of his treasures.

"Many magnificent artists have turned to commercial art to put food on their table." In the entry way there is a framed advertisement for Cream of Wheat, drawn by Li'l Abner's creator Al Capp. After Al Capp's death, his widow married the father of one of Lou's close friends. When visiting the Greenstein home in North Reading, the former Mrs. Capp was quite surprised to see Capp's Cream of Wheat artwork; she had not known her husband produced such commercial art.

In the hallway across from his 200 meat grinders, Lou has a collection of Cream of Wheat ads from 1905–1925. The content of some seemingly politically incorrect today, these ads mirror a different generation.

We move on to a saltwater taffy-pull machine, rescued from behind stairs in a Winthrop house slated for demolition, which turned out to have been a saltwater taffy store. On the floor a rack holds perhaps twenty rolling pins, glass and wooden. People used to fill the glass ones with cold water to expedite the rolling of pie crust. In the corner of his test kitchen, Lou directs our attention to his complete collection of *Art Culinaire,* a hard-covered magazine that began publication in the 1950s. Having found them at a yard sale, Lou also has the very first edition of *Gourmet* magazine along with all the issues of the first four years, beginning in the 1940s.

Why does Lou collect these kitchen things? "My collecting of menus started in childhood. I guess you'd say we were lower-lower income growing up in Revere. My mother was a phenomenal cook. We didn't really know we were poor. Mother made skim milk out of powdered milk."

"Dad also cooked some. His specialty was kippers and eggs. I still love that smell." As a distributor of provisions and meats, Lou's father knew the markets and joked with the men who worked there. Young Lou often accompanied his father to Haymarket. "It was a nice experience as a child."

On Sundays, for a special treat, the Greensteins usually left Revere and went out to dinner. It was on these excursions that Lou began to collect menus. In 1992, PBC International published *A La Carte, a Tour of Dining History* by Lou Greenstein. Chosen from the 4,000 to 5,000 menus in his collection, the menus pictured and described in this book date from the 1860s to the 1960s and represent meals served on trains, ships, special holidays, political and patriotic events. "Of course I did not personally collect the ones from the 1860s," he said with a laugh.

From July 25, 1927, we find the menu commemorating Colonel Charles A. Lindberg's transatlantic flight. Celebrating the building of the Brooklyn Bridge, the golden anniversary tri-fold dinner menu on May 24, 1933, appears on page 115. Valentine's Day celebrations began in the early 1880s; through menus we learn how restaurants quickly picked up on this romantic holiday. A Thanksgiving Day menu from 1875 features eleven different styles of oysters and five varieties of native duck. A complete dinner at Boston's Hotel Brunswick on November 25, 1926, cost $3.50, including scallop Newburg and six vegetables, as well as the traditional turkey or duck.

Thomas Aageson, now past president of the Mystic Seaport Museum Stores, says in his introduction to *A La Carte,* "Lou Greenstein spent years, and a lot of money to collect and preserve these menus. He did it neither for profit, nor to write this book, but out of love of what these menus represent to culinary history and to American history."

Just prior to the publication of *A La Carte,* Mystic Seaport hired Lou to help them research and document the breads and cookies in their historic bakery to reflect baked goods of the late 1800s. A small cookbook, *Recipe Sampler,* resulted. Because the bake shop was using a state-of-the-art conveyer belt oven, Lou needed to test recipes, rewriting them so they had the taste of 1880 to 1890. He reworked the recipes for the souvenir cookbook yet again to insure early Americana results in 1990s ovens at home.

The booklet contains a short history of each kind of cookie and bread.

For example "Joe Froggers" originated in Marblehead, Massachusetts. Legend has it that "Old Black Joe" baked these cookies, as plump as the fat little frogs in the pond nearby. Fishermen would trade a jug of rum for a batch because the cookies kept so well at sea, the ginger and spices in them warding off seasickness.

Also in the *Mystic Seaport Recipe Sampler* we find that Mrs. E. E. Kellogg, of later cereal fame, published the first recipe for peanut butter on page 395 of her 1892 cookbook, *Science in the Kitchen*. At the time she was developing a new system of cookery based on healthy consumption of grains, fruits, vegetables and nuts, encouraging people to limit their consumption of animal meats and fats. Sound familiar?

In addition to these two books, Lou wrote a cookbook for the Braun Company featuring its hand-held blender. Gillette purchased this German company and subsequently introduced the popular European kitchen gadget for which Lou devised recipes.

In another project, he acted as a culinary consultant to revamp the restaurant at Fruitlands in Harvard, Massachusetts, the place where Bronson Alcott, father of Louisa May, established a utopian community in 1843 committed to eating only uncooked vegetables.

With a degree from hotel and restaurant management from the University of Massachusetts at Amherst, Lou's primary job is director of auxiliary services at New Hampshire College in Manchester. He overseas the food service, the bookstores and the campus vending machines for this college, which has a resident population of 1,000.

Does he make any money from his collections? "Sometimes I buy on speculation. I have an affinity to Russian objects. I recently purchased a Russian naval cap for a dollar and sold it this week on E-bay [an Internet auction site] for fifteen," he said. With a digital camera Lou photographs, for example, the 1950 Weave Ware ice tea set or the Ayers-Sarsaparilla tray, and downloads the pictures to his computer. He sets a minimum bid, and then for seven days the picture of his object and his e-mail address appear on www.ebay.com.

"One collects with the hope of wealth," said Lou. "One time I paid fifteen dollars for a few pieces of cast iron that I later discovered were worth close to $2,500." Lou sees the yard sale as a valid recycling format. "If you need something, inevitably you can find it," he said.

Lou also collects because he loves learning about the history of these objects. "Collecting makes you do research. You learn a lot. I have boxes of books about glass, utensils and cast iron."

From 1979 until 1994 when the show went off the air, Lou was the chef on Channel 5's "Good Day Show" with Eileen Prose and John Willis. For five years following the "Good Day Show," Lou was the chef historian on "Cookin' USA" out of Nashville, Tennessee. "I would fly down there with a trunk of antique gadgets and tape six shows at a time. It was great fun. I was sorry the show ended," he said.

His name appearing on the credits for "Mrs. Field's Cooking Americana," Lou also has researched the historical content for the famous cookie lady's show on Channel 2. Lou has written food columns about preparing a meal for under $20 for the *Lawrence Eagle-Tribune,* and features for the *Hartford Current* on food topics as unique as the mighty chestnut. He thoroughly enjoys lecturing fifteen to twenty times per year at garden clubs and historical societies about his collections and about culinary history. Audience members often bring unusual kitchen gadgets for discussion or appraisal.

Picking out a favorite object from his collection, a sausage stuffer the size of a baseball bat, he chuckled at its having been the source of an embarrassing moment for Susan Wornick when he demonstrated its use for her on the "Good Day Show" some years ago. A clip of this same moment subsequently appeared on the "Oprah Winfrey Show."

When asked his favorite food, Lou did not take long to answer. "Peasant food. When people don't have a great deal to work with they must take the basic ingredients and turn them into something wonderful. This is the real test of a cook," he said.

—November 5, 1999

Ken Thomson, Cyclist

"I was forty years old when I started serious riding," said Ken Thomson of his biking career. "Beth, did we ever not have a bicycle?" he calls to his wife who is heading down the cellar stairs after putting on her shoes that clip into the pedals, and her bike helmet, which has an attached rear view mirror similar to one a dentist uses to look at molars.

Ken acquired his first bike, one with balloon tires, when he lived in rural Pompton Plains, New Jersey. "I could never really run or walk comfortably after I had polio at age seven," said Ken. In the 1950s, he had an English three-speed. "It was a big deal to have gears—awesome." Multispeed bicycles having been invented in France in 1936, Europeans had been using derailleurs for decades. Ken and his wife bought their first derailleur bikes in 1963, just as this kind of bike was beginning to become popular in the United States. In 1966 the Thomsons moved to Marblehead Street in North Reading, but it was not until July 3, 1970, that their neighbor Bob McKown, a U. S. Cycling Federation (USCF) member and serious racer, convinced them to attend a criterium (crit) race with him in Fitchburg, Massachusetts, as spectators.

There are basically three kinds of serious road-bike races:
- The criterium is a race on a small course of one or two miles per lap with many loops, and fun for spectators to watch,
- The time trial is a standard twenty-four mile race, and
- The point to point race is usually fifty or sixty miles.

Off-road or dirt (mountain) bike races are a different sport altogether, as are marathon events like the AIDS Ride from Boston to New York City in September.

Ken has recently assembled a bicycle for a Malden man, Danny Valez-Rivera, who is training for the AIDS Ride next fall. Another North Reading resident, John Wiklanski, made the 300-mile, three-day trek in the fall of 1997. Raising $7,000 for AIDS research, John was second highest in Boston pledges for the event that year. Three thousand riders participated.

In the mid-1980s, Ken rode 130 miles in a race from Boston to Provincetown. "It's an old man's dream to do that one again," he said. Because he had counted on stopping more than twice to drink and eat on the eight-hour ride, his twenty-ounce water bottle ran dry. "I was as weak as a kitten," he said. "Once you get hungry or thirsty it is too late." In hot weather Ken recommends drinking twenty ounces of water every hour and eating a banana every thirty miles. "There are one banana, two banana and three banana rides." One of his favorite biking snacks is little, boiled, red potatoes.

The group that race to Provincetown go once in the spring and once in the fall. This race is at a very fast pace, with a rigid tempo of circulating the front riders so that the work of cutting the wind is shared equally. Twenty miles per hour was a good speed for Ken in the 1970s and 1980s. CCB (Cycle Club Basingstoke), a racing club out of Ipswich with which he has long been affiliated, averages twenty-four miles per hour. This group rides from the Batchelder School parking lot every Tuesday evening at 6:00 P.M. from April to October and on Wednesday evenings from Topsfield center. You've seen these Lycra-clad racers screaming up Haverhill Street at dusk. "Air resistance goes up as the cube of your speed," said Ken. "If you double your speed, you multiply your wind resistance by a factor of eight. So a little faster is a lot more work."

The comfort and design of the bike you ride is at the core of your success as a racer, but also key if you tour. "The difference between a bike that fits or not is like clothing or a shoe that does not fit—torture. You should be able to ride all day without pain," said Ken. Made by a California company, with a 1970s-racing frame, his bike is a Rivendell, named after a fantasy place in *The Hobbit*. "I would no more use somebody else's bike than use somebody else's toothbrush," he said. It takes years to get your bike "tweaked" exactly so that it fits you. Present day racing bikes, in Ken's opinion, are designed for speed only, not comfort. Essentially crit bikes, modern racing bikes have a rear wheel very close to the seat stay, and a shorter chain. "It makes for twitchy steering."

Not only a rider, Ken has a long and illustrious career as a bike mechanic. A teacher of French and German at Wakefield High School since 1966, Ken has spent many summers working as a bike mechanic, first at the North Reading Cycle Shop, which used to be next to the Hornet's Nest, then at Northeast Bikes in Saugus, Pedal Power in Exeter, New Hampshire, owned by Ken's former neighbor

Bob McKown, and, most recently, at Belmont Wheelworks. Since his heart problems in the early 1990s and open-heart surgery last winter, he prefers to repair bikes in his basement. In the past fifteen years, Ken has repaired bicycles from the lowly Huffy to the lofty Merlin, a titanium frame bike worth about $4,000.

Ken's bike repair business also has a community service component. "Ever since his daughter Jen raced on the Phillips Academy Cycling Team, Ken has been particularly keen on getting women going in the sport," said Henry Wilmer, one of Phillips Academy's cycling coaches. "He loves to see kids try it." Five of the ten students on the Academy's cycling team are riding bikes Ken supplied.

"He tends the stable," adds Derek Williams, founder of the Phillips Academy cycling team in 1980. From 1986 through 1988, he and Henry coached Ken's daughter. "Ken finds the horses others might give up for broken. His help has been instrumental in keeping the team going. Every year he adds more quantity and quality," said Derek. With competitive racing bikes selling for $1,000, students are not likely to make such an investment when they are not even sure they will make the team.

"I did not start supplying bikes to the team until after Jen graduated. I saw what the sport did for her self-image." He wanted to extend the opportunity to other young people. Not all the bikes cost Ken $1,000. He has gotten good bikes and bike parts from liquidation sales, and he is constantly watching the *Want Advertiser* for deals.

In her last year at Phillips Academy, Jen received her USCF license and did some serious racing during the summer. In the 1988 Fitchburg race, the same race Ken and Beth had attended with their neighbor twenty years earlier, Jen placed in the top ten. At Smith College, where she went that fall, there was no cycling team; Jen trained with the University of Massachusetts Amherst team, and in the spring of 1990, qualified for the National Collegiate Competition in Colorado Springs. "I took time off from teaching," remembers Ken. "She had no team—I was her mechanic and companion."

Being a competent mechanic comes in handy for long bicycle trips. His French and German "quite adequate," a six-week European tour in 1993 did not seem at all formidable, even with his newly diagnosed heart condition. With his own personal nurse Beth on her purple Bridgestone X01 at his side, Ken set out from Munich where their son, Josh lives, to Southern Bavaria and Rheingau, staying at bed and breakfasts, called *Zimmer frei* in Germany. "We had no itinerary at all—just went as the spirit moved us," recalled Ken. "After traveling up the Mosel River to Trier, we went into the Alsace area of France.

Two years later, Ken and Beth took a two-week guided tour of the Czech Republic on bicycles. There were ten in the tour that started in Prague and pedaled to Bratislava, the capital of Slovakia on the Danube. "I would not have wanted to tour in the Czech Republic without a guide because of the language issues," said Ken. To return to Europe on another bike tour, perhaps the Loire River Valley, is an attainable dream for Ken and his wife—something they hope to do.

In the meantime, as the good weather arrives in New England, Ken looks forward to the twenty-mile ride around Cape Ann from Gloucester to Rockport and back. "We mosey," said Ken. "A good rider can do that in an hour, but we take three. We stop at the end of Bearskin Neck for strudel."

Beth is coming up the basement stairs, peeling off her padded, fingerless gloves, having finished her afternoon ride through the Harold Parker Forest adjacent to their home. "What's the name of that strudel place, Beth?" he calls to his wife. "Hemuth's Coffee Shop, I think," Ken mutters, in answer to his own question.

—April 13, 1999

Katharine Barr and Billie Downing, Ninety-Nines Aviators

During the summer of 1999, on the first United States space flight commanded by a woman, Space Shuttle Columbia's astronauts flawlessly released the world's most powerful X-ray telescope into orbit. At the helm of the craft was Air Force Colonel Eileen Collins, a longtime member of the Ninety-Nines. An aeronautic organization exclusively for female pilots, the Ninety-Nines are all "Sisters of the Sky."

Two members, Billie Downing and Katharine Barr, live right here in North Reading.

Billie Downing began her flying lessons in California in 1962. She had been interested in learning to fly after her first excursion in a light plane in San Antonio, Texas, with a young flight engineer, Stu, who later became her husband. Billie left the Southwest in 1965 and, soon after, with her husband bought land off Haverhill Street in North Reading. After the couple heard about a house that was slated for demolition as part of the Reading Baptist Church renovation, they were able to purchase it and move it to the Gowing strawberry farm. They still call this place home.

Working for the Air Force at Hanscom Field as an electronics buyer, a position she held for thirteen years, Billie continued her pilot's training in Massachusetts. She earned her license in 1967. At the Arrow Club at Hanscom Field, Bedford, Billie's instructor, Bob Bugg assured her, "As soon as you get your license, my wife, Pamela, is taking you to a Ninety-Nines meeting." Billie has been an active member since March 1968, holding almost all chapter and section offices, including sectional governor from 1982 to 1984.

While she has participated in local air rallies and won first place as copilot in three of these competitions, Billie and her husband fly primarily for the sheer joy of it, and for travel. "I have several thousand hours of copiloting and probably 500 hours of flying as pilot-in-command. I never tire of it. This land is so beautiful from the air. And every state is different," said Billie.

As a young woman growing up in upstate New York Katharine Barr dreamed of being a pilot. The summer she turned fifteen, her father, a country lawyer, paid for a few half-hour flying lessons at the one-runway Oneonta Airport. The hobby proved to be too expensive, however, and Katharine returned to competitive archery.

Thirty-four years later, in 1988, Katharine was highest bidder on one flying lesson offered at a Treble Chorus of New England fund-raising auction. For $60 she purchased her first Lawrence Airport flying lesson with Al Croteau, a Treble Chorus dad. Al had three or four flying students at the time and worked full time at General Electric in Lynn.

"For the next two years I was taking lessons in Al's Cessna 172 as often as the weather, our schedules and my budget would allow," said Katharine.

On July 10, 1990, she passed her FAA test, earning her wings. "I mailed off my application to Ninety-Nines the next day," she said.

From her friend Billie, Katharine knew of the Ninety-Nines organization, founded in 1929 by Amelia Earhart in Valley Stream, New York. Membership was then, and is still, open to any woman with a pilot's license; the purpose of the organization is "good fellowship, jobs, a central office and files on women in aviation."

At that first meeting, according to the *History of the Ninety-Nines, Inc.,* founding members proposed names like The Climbing Vines, Noisy Birdwomen and Homing Pigeons. Amelia Earhart and Jean Davis Hoyt put a stop to that nonsense, suggesting the name be taken from the sum total of charter members—ninety-nine in all. And so it was. Now the membership exceeds 6,000 worldwide.

Two hundred thirty female pilots, their spouses and guests attended the annual Ninety-Nines convention from which Billie and Katharine have just returned. Held this year in Oklahoma City from July 21 to 25 at the Will Rogers International Airport headquarters, this educational gathering featured an annual meeting, the Amelia Earhart Annual Scholarship luncheon, and presentations by the Federal Aviation Association and the Airline Pilots Association.

The big event of this year's convention was the dedication of the Museum of Women Pilots that occupies the second floor of the group's headquarters. "It is the definitive history of women in the air, with artifacts, uniforms, trophies and photos," said Katharine. "Thousands came to the dedication." There have been thirty-one conventions since Billie became a member of Ninety-Nines. "I missed one convention in Australia and a few in the 1980s. I've probably attended over twenty-five," she said.

Billie and Katharine have shared their love of flying and their loyalty to the Ninety-Nines organization on many occasions. Shortly after Katharine earned her license, the Downings invited her to accompany them from Kenosha, Wisconsin, to Oakland, California, in a Cessna 172.

"I had never thought of doing anything as magical as that," said Katharine. "To see the country from 2,000 feet was awesome in the true sense of the word ... If I never flew another mile ... it was the trip of a lifetime. For miles you did not see a sign of human habitation."

The Downings generally fly once a week in a borrowed Cessna 172, perhaps to have lunch in North Adams or Block Island. For seventeen years they owned their own Cessna. After they sold it, they had their own vacation of a lifetime, renting a small plane in Australia. In a detailed account in the *Aero Club of New England* newsletter, their flying friends from Princeton, Hal and Michelee Cabot, recounted the thirteen-day aerial safari in the Outback. Five planes and ten people flew over billibongs, kangaroos, Ayers Rock, and the spot where Banjo Paterson wrote "Waltzing Matilda."

Crystal-clear days were perfect for flying, but language was occasionally a problem. "Our greatest moment of confusion came when a coastal sector controller told us to report at Cudgen Lake, which came out "like." So we spent several anxious moments looking for Cudgen Light—which doesn't exist," said Hal.

Katharine is the governor of the New England section of Ninety-Nines, a two-year position. In addition to those duties, which take her to five meetings in Oklahoma City, she serves on the newly formed New England Advisory Board to The Dulles Center, a Smithsonian offshoot of the National Air and Space Museum just outside Washington, D.C.

If that is not enough, she has assumed a major role in the 2000 Air Race Classic; she is co-chair of the "terminus" events at the Hyannis/Barnstable County Airport on June 23–25, 2000. Departing from Tucson, Arizona, on June 20, 2000, fifty or more planes, piloted and copiloted by more than 100 female aviators, will follow the transcontinental traditional begun by their sisters in 1927.

Originally flown in antique biplanes, and piloted by women in leather helmets and long white silk scarves, the most famous participants of that day included Amelia Earhart and Louise Thaden. At the first race, Western comic Will Rogers was on hand for the lineup and dubbed the event the "Powder Puff Derby," a name that stuck until the more politically correct 1970s when it was reestablished as the Air Race Classic. In 1999, Air Race Classic gave its top cash prize of $5,000 to pilot Denise A. Waters of New York and her copilot Bonnie Porter, an elementary school art teacher in Haverhill, Massachusetts, who is an active member of Billie and Katharine's Ninety-Nines chapter.

—August 1, 1999

Steve Perkins, Gloucester Fisherman

The codfish, mainstay of Massachusetts's economy for centuries, is in danger, and Steve Perkins of North Reading, a Gloucester fisherman, is worried. Like his brother, father, grandfather and great-grandfather, Steve makes his living from the sea.

Growing up in Perkins Cove, Maine, Steve's earliest memories are of helping the men in his family to lobster. "I started going when I was five or six years old. They always gave me a job I could do." Steve had his own sixteen-foot open lobster boat when he was in high school. While attending college at University of New Hampshire, where he studied psychology and education, Steve had a partnership with his father on a larger boat. After teaching for a year at New Market High School, he heard the call of the ocean again, and decided to make fishing his vocation.

A move to North Reading with his wife, Judith, and two children in the 1980s made fishing out of the Maine harbor difficult; Steve relocated his two boats, the *Danielle Rose* and the *David James* to Gloucester. Named after his son, the *David James* is sixty-seven feet and weighs 100 tons. The craft is literally a half-a-million dollar factory, capable of holding 50,000 to 60,000 pounds of iced fish.

Before going out to sea in the summer Steve stocks her with fifteen tons of crushed ice. "In the winter we don't need quite so much ice," he said with a smile. Bringing home 10,000 pounds of fish is a typical haul. Steve sells all his fish to one customer: the Pigeon Cove Fish Company owned by Bread and Circus food store chain. "I usually stay with one outfit for a long time. Bread and Circus wants fabulous quality, and they are willing to pay a little more for it. I run that kind of business."

Built for scalloping or bottom fishing, the *David James* can sleep seven. Steve typically takes a crew of three: Joe Black, who does all the cooking, Scottie, and himself. The three men cook and sleep in the forecastle in the bow. The wheelhouse is also forward, but above deck. The rest of the ship is engine room and fish hole.

"We're on call all the time. On a moment's notice we go for seven days at this time of year, longer in the summer. You watch the weather all the time. On the whole, the predictions are pretty reliable." Has he seen bad weather like that portrayed in the currently popular book by Sebastian Junger, *The Perfect Storm*?

"Anyone who has spent any time on the ocean has had close calls. If you haven't been frightened at one time or another, you don't have a brain," said Steve. "You have to know every inch of your boat, and keep it up; the boat is the only thing between you and the elements."

Named for his daughter, the *Danielle Rose* was a fifty-four foot, seventy-ton ship. In July 1996, Steve sold this second boat to the U. S. government and, sadly, a perfectly fine ship got scraped. Why was that?

In *The Perfect Storm,* Sebastian Junger explains how haddock "landings" in the late 1980s plummeted to one-fiftieth of what they had been in 1960, and cod "landings" dropped by a factor of four.

"The culprit," explained the book, "was a sudden change in technology ... New quick-freeze techniques allowed enormous Russian factory ships ... to scour the bottom with nets that could take thirty tons of fish in a single haul." Overfishing decimated the marine populations.

In 1976, the Magnuson Fishery Conservation and Management Act extended our national sovereignty to 200 miles off shore. Foreign fishing vessels could no longer fish these waters. "Within three years," continues Junger's book, "the New England fleet had doubled to 1,300 boats." In 1988, a Chatham fisherman, Mark Simonitsch stood to speak at a New England Fisheries Council meeting, suggesting Georges Bank be closed to all fishing.

"There were big problems with the biomass in the Gulf of Maine," said Steve. "The cod population was desperately low and so fragile it could fail. Georges Bank cod—same problem."

Under the Department of Commerce, the National Oceanic and Atmospheric Administration, (NOAA), begun restricting how much fishing could occur. Areas of Georges Bank were closed at certain times. Mesh size of nets, and size of fish by species had been strictly monitored since 1985. But now boats had to have a sailing number before they left the harbor and a landing number for their return. The government began to curtail the number of days one could fish.

Neither choice desirable, some boat captains took "fleet days at sea" to have their fishing days at sea reduced by fifty percent in three years. Another option was "individual days at sea," which might give more fishing time based on the history and productivity of the boat. As a result of the restrictions, the *David James* may now fish only 157 days per year, and the *Danielle Rose* is gone.

"As fishermen we used to have so much freedom," said Steve. "If you wanted to take a big risk, you could make good money. It was very individual. Now it is so regulated. The bad boys who were in it for the fast buck are gone."

The government restricts Steve to 400 pounds of cod per day. In February that limit may be reduced to 100 pounds or maybe even go to zero. The fishermen know 1999 will see drastic cuts. "All fishing disturbs the ecosystem to some degree, but everyone wants to find seafood on the menu," said Steve.

Taking away a primary species like the cod puts pressure on the other species. To catch schools of herring takes sophisticated equipment, and the technology makes it quite successful. But if herring or shrimp are overfished because of the cod restrictions, what are the ground fish to feed on? "We have a bad cycle here," said Steve. "You can't manage one resource without affecting another."

Steve repeatedly brings up the issue of pollution. "When I was a kid there were no sewer outfalls. Now every town pumps it out, treated with chlorine. Fish no longer return to places near the Maine Coast where I saw them all my life. I don't think it is all from overfishing. Mesh restrictions are not new."

Steve sees plastic bags all through the Gulf of Maine. Seventy-five miles to sea, and 150 fathoms deep, the *David James* typically pulls up ten plastic bags a trip.

"There isn't that much floating trash. People are conscientious about bringing trash in to shore and putting it in the Dumpster. Then the local garbage contractor takes it to a company that puts it on a barge and takes it out to dump in the sea!" he lamented.

Sylvia Earle, a marine biologist interviewed December 12, 1998, in the *Boston Globe* expressed Steve's concern. "The ocean is the ultimate sewer for human society ... What we put on our lawns, golf courses, fields and farms flows through groundwater into rivers and, ultimately, the ocean." Steve believes Earle has put her finger right on the issue. "It's not just rocks and water out there, but a living minestrone, top to bottom. It shapes the chemistry of our planet ... We're trying to tell fishermen how many fish it's safe to take, and we don't even know how many there are to start with," she wrote.

Five years ago Steve Perkins would have said the hardest thing about his job was the weather. "But there is good weather, too," he said. Endlessly complex and constantly changing, government regulation is the biggest challenge for the fisherman today. "I'm not blaming the government. It's a complex problem. But this is a man's livelihood, and it is difficult to plan for the future. I don't see the government ever stepping back."

—January 22, 1999

Jack Vasapoli, Sculptor and Sax Player in Tabasco Fiasco

Eighteen years ago in San Francisco, Jack Vasapoli acquired his first alto sax as partial payment for building Jack Friar's redwood deck. Twelve years ago he picked up the horn and took some lessons in Wakefield from Berklee graduate Tony Viola, who used to play with Glenn Miller. Today, Jack is Juan El Mundo, vocalist and sax player in Tabasco Fiasco, a group that performs regularly at the Horseshoe Café, Palmers, J. Rags, and Strange Brew.

Every summer this six-piece band plays rhythm and blues, swing, rock, Tex/Mex, soul and funk at the Ipswich River Park's regular Wednesday night barbecue. "This is our third year at the park. A friend of mine brings down some antique cars and parks them behind us to show how old we are in relation to the cars. 'Hey, look at this one. The horn still works,'" Jack says with a laugh.

When he first picked up the sax, his wife, Joyce, was teaching at Red Sneakers preschool in Reading. Jack began jamming with Kitt Cox, one of the teachers there. At the time Jack also frequented the Horseshoe Café. "That's where I met Jim Bennett from North Andover and Jeff Edwards (Droesch)."

"I was interested in accordion roots music," says Jeff Edwards, "especially Louisiana Cajun and Zydeco. Jack had spent some time in California where he was exposed to Tex/Mex groups like Los Lobos and Linda Ronstadt."

Encouraging audience participation, the philosophy of Jeff's group, Jumpin' George and the Blue Lights, was to make everyone welcome. The idea was to create a congregational spirit similar to Preacher Jack, the rock-a-billy piano player from Salem whose mission it is to get everyone involved.

"Jack Vasapoli knew *Cielito Lindo,*" remembers Jeff Edwards. "He was shy at first, but I was able to get him on stage to sing that song. He really captured the spirit of the material. He has a natural charisma. He'd wear this shiny red jacket. Loud. He had a Latin flair."

The other North Reading member of Tabasco Fiasco, Paul Lewis, alias Swami Lewis, adds that Jack has "something you can't learn." Jack has the sound, the feeling for the music, the ear.

Over the past ten years Tabasco Fiasco has played college gigs at Holy Cross, Bates and Bentley. In June they played a benefit in Methuen at the Knights of Columbus, proceeds to go to the Multiple Sclerosis Society and Homeless Veterans. "I made eyeglasses for this guy Dave Perna who was running the benefit. They approached us. We don't really do this for the money. It might as well be going to a good cause," says Jack.

By day, Jack is an optician, grinding lenses and fitting glasses with his brother, Paul, in the family business in Melrose. "I've always liked the lab work best," says Jack. For a time he ran Family Opticians in Reading. That store went out of business in October of 1998. "Retail is not me," he says. Working with his brother pays the bills so that Jack can enjoy the band, and pursue another passion, sculpture.

A bio-chem major at Suffolk University, Jack graduated in 1972 and taught public school science at Wakefield High School and in Hillsboro, New Hampshire. It was in 1972 while he was working as a short-order cook at Lums Restaurant in Saugus that he first met Joyce Quinlan, a waitress there. For him it was love at first sight. "We ran away together to the Florida Keys, to the Cape, to Europe, and then to Ontario where Joyce taught macramé, and I taught silk-screening and leather work."

For a time they lived in Boulder, Colorado, where Joyce studied tai chi at Naropa, a Tibetan Buddhist college, and Jack took Tibetan woodcarving. Finally, the Vasapolis settled in San

Francisco where Jack studied Tibetan Thangka painting at Nygimpa, a Buddhist college in Berkeley.

"I should have gone to art school," says Jack. "My Melrose High School art teacher, Paul Squatrito, really turned me on to it."

During their eight years in California, Jack and Joyce both did some teaching. With Governor Ronald Reagan's Proposition Three educational cutbacks, Jack did not see prospects for a permanent teaching job. To pay the bills he took a full-time carpentry position with Dr. Reidar Wennesland, an elderly Norwegian who owned three houses on San Francisco's exclusive Potrero Hill. Two of the houses were inhabited by the doctor's six monkeys, five dogs and six kinkajous (honeybears from Central America, the size of small raccoons). The third house, where Reidar lived, had an extensive sculpture garden and a sizeable collection of American abstract art.

Formerly a ship's doctor, Reidar also had been a doctor to North Beach street people in the late '60s including poet Allen Ginsberg. "I worked for Reidar for two or three years," says Jack, "sometimes taking my salary in Thangkas, which I could not bear to see the monkeys shred." The monkeys would destroy the houses; Jack would repair them. It was a full-time job.

In 1980, Oscar, the rhesus monkey, got loose and bit a prominent Potrero Hill woman on the leg. Lacking permits for his exotic pets, and fearing confiscation by the authorities, Reidar employed Jack to rent a trailer and two vans, complete with CBs, to transport the animals to British Columbia where Reidar's brother lived. Reidar led the way, singing opera arias over the CB to entertain himself.

"This was an underground thing. We had two spider monkeys, two rhesus monkeys, one woolly monkey, six kinkajous, a Great Dane, a French poodle and a mutt. When we stopped at a sleazy little motel in Bellingham, Washington, the man at the desk asked, 'Got any pets?' 'A few,' I said."

In British Columbia, Reidar was not able to obtain the permits to keep his unusual pets, and eventually the monkeys and kinkajous ended up at the British Columbia zoo. Reidar returned to San Francisco with his dogs.

So, why is there a Great Dane-sized bronze rhesus monkey in the Vasapoli living room on Marblehead Street, North Reading? Having saved his pet monkeys from animal research laboratories, Dr. Wennesland commissioned Jack to create a bronze of the doctor's head next to the head of one of his monkeys. Pleased with the work, Reidar proposed a full-sized bronze monkey honoring the contribution of monkeys to medical science. Reidar planned to donate Jack's work to the Oakland Art Museum. Seeing an artistic opportunity offering professional visibility, Jack decided to donate his time, a mere two years or so, Reidar paying the foundry costs of $3,000.

The sculpture finished, Reidar changed his mind and wanted to keep the work for his own sculpture garden. The sculpture being worth closer to $12,000, Jack refused to let it go for the foundry costs alone. "I had to work in the foundry for a few months to pay off my debt. It was a very toxic place, but I got good experience as an apprentice."

Although the busts of his two Sicilian grandfathers, Vincenzo and Philip, are bronze, most of Jack's recent work is wood. It took him three years to carve the red, yellow and orange phoenix rising out of a wrought-iron ash pit near his breakfast table. "Too many feathers! That's my last feather job," he says.

Jack carved the slender four-foot-high baritone-saxophone player out of walnut. For the horn he used osage, a hard wood from Maryland, which his neighbor Jen Pieper supplies for him.

The serene face of his wife, with oak curls flying recklessly, has a mirror behind, which surprisingly reveals Jack's self-portrait in relief.

Almost complete is the copy of a Notre Dame gargoyle crouched in the shed where Tabasco Fiasco rehearses. Out past the vegetable garden, past the fishpond and the dog run, this small dwelling, the scene of band rehearsals every second Thursday at 7:30 P.M., is also Jack's space to carve.

Jeff Edwards, who left Tabasco Fiasco a year ago, asked, "Is Jack still doing his whistling solo in 'Shuckin' and A-Jivin'? That one song about summed it up for all of us. I miss my association with him more than I miss the music. I don't think I can throw enough flowers in his direction."

—July 7, 2000

About the Author and the Artist

Winner in college of the F. L. Hunt Poetry Award, Nancy Bailey Miller's first collection of poetry, *Dance Me Along the Path,* was published in 1997. Her poems have appeared in anthologies and magazines including *Ancient Paths* (2001), *Blue Unicorn* (1998 and 2001), *Pine Island Journal of New England Poetry* (1998), *Voices* (1997), *Pleiades ArtsNorth* (1997), *Our Mothers, Our Selves* (1996), *Landscapes & Legends: Poems for the Andovers* (1996), and *Mediphors* (1994). She has taken writing workshops with Sharon Olds, Rafael Campo, and Liz Rosenberg among others.

A teacher of English in the Phillips Academy summer session, and of Suzuki violin, she is also the office manager of Cochran Chapel at the academy. She writes a column for *Town Crossings,* a publication of the *Lawrence Eagle-Tribune,* from which the stories in this book are taken.

A native of White Plains, New York, she has lived for thirty-two years in North Reading, Massachusetts. She loves Brahms, peppermint stick ice cream and waterslides.

* * * *

Louise Anderson of North Reading is a graduate of the Art Institute of Boston. She has studied with Alfred Tulk and Hilda Levy of New Haven, Connecticut. While living there, she taught at the Creative Arts Workshop.

Her course "Beginning Watercolorists" has won great acceptance in the area. Presently, she is teaching at The Arts Center in Wilmington and also in North Reading.

As an active member of Andover's Artists Guild and the Lynnfield Art Guild, her paintings have been exhibited in many group and one-man shows. Her work has won numerous awards and is included in private and corporate collections.